Tough Justice

Sentencing and Penal Policies in the 1990s

For Helen and Sally

Tough Justice

Sentencing and Penal Policies in the 1990s

Ian Dunbar

and

Anthony Langdon

BLACKSTONE
PRESS LIMITED

First Published in Great Britain 1998 by Blackstone Press Limited,
Aldine Place, London W12 8AA. Telephone: 0181-740 2277

© I. Dunbar, A. Langdon, 1998

ISBN: 1 85431 725 3

British Library Cataloguing in Publication Data
A CIP catalogue record for this book is available from the British Library

Typeset by Style Photosetting Ltd, Mayfield, East Sussex
Printed Livesey Ltd, Shrewsbury, Shropshire

Contents

Acknowledgements

The opinions in this book are our own but we are grateful to all the busy people who pointed us to information and gave us their views.

Andrew Ashworth, David Downes and Rod Morgan not only gave us their time but also let us have advance copies of their forthcoming publications, and we are particularly grateful to them.

Among the others who helped us we want to record our special thanks to Keith Bottomley, Anthony Bottoms, Elizabeth Burney, Silvia Casale, Paul Cavadino, David Faulkner, Adrian Grounds, Alison Liebling, Marc Mauer, Andrew Rutherford, Stephen Shaw, Vivien Stern, Roger Tarling, David Thomas and John Vagg.

The library of the Institute of Criminology, Cambridge, went to much trouble to help us, and we are particularly grateful to the librarian, Helen Krarup.

1 Introduction

Crime has risen remorselessly for more than a generation, and it is quite right that the public should be deeply concerned. Much of that concern has now been channelled toward the greater use of prison as the main response. This book is about the grave problems already being created by the scale of imprisonment in this country, and the reasons for believing that prison expansion is not a sensible approach to the protection of the public.

When the Criminal Justice Act 1991 received royal assent it seemed a watershed, establishing sentencing principles that would endure for years to come. It had been prepared over the previous four years with unusually elaborate consultation and documentation that set out the government's central thesis that punishment should be awarded according to the test of 'just deserts'.

After decades of generally ineffective attempts to moderate the use of imprisonment and to get a better balance between the number of prisoners and the available prison accommodation, it seemed in 1991 as though that goal might at last be attained and underpinned on stable foundations. The prison building programme was making thousands of new places available for use, and the new Act set the courts' sentencing powers within a framework of provisions that required them to consider all alternative disposals before sending an offender to prison. In parallel with the Act action was in hand to tighten the management of non-custodial disposals so that they delivered a system of 'punishment in the community' that would command the confidence of sentencers and, in order to strengthen the credibility of fines as an alternative penalty, the Act established a system of means-related fines in magistrates' courts. Parole and early release, which had become riddled with anomalies, were re-established on a secure basis.

Yet this meticulously crafted interlocking structure began to fall to pieces almost at once. By the summer of 1993 the judges had complained so effectively about some of the ways in which it restricted their sentencing powers that the Home Secretary, Kenneth Clarke, had promised legislation to repeal those provisions, along with the whole of the new system for means-related fines, where there had been some absurd and well-publicised anomalies. A few months later, in October 1993, the next Home Secretary, Michael Howard, used the Conservative Party conference to repudiate the long evolution of criminal justice policy, which he described as too far tilted in favour of the criminal and against the protection of the public. He went out of his way to claim that the 27 measures that he announced would mean more people in prison but said, 'I do not flinch from that. We shall no longer judge the success of our system of justice by a fall in our prison population.' He encapsulated his approach, and distanced himself from the previous consensus, with the simple phrase, 'Prison works'.

Two years later, in October 1995, Michael Howard announced to the Conservative Party conference that he proposed to introduce legislation that would scrap the parole scheme entirely and would require the courts to impose mandatory terms of imprisonment on various categories of repeat offenders. That legislation — the Crime (Sentences) Act 1997 — ran into an unprecedented depth and vehemence of opposition from the Lord Chief Justice and other judges in the House of Lords immediately before the general election in 1997. Both penal policy and relations between government and judiciary had been changed far more within the lifetime of the Major administration than had happened at any of the changes of government since the end of the Second World War, at least.

For a government to make such a complete and sudden reversal of policy is extraordinary by any standards but on this occasion it was made even more remarkable by the fact that the main opposition party followed the government's lead throughout. Having criticised the 1991 Act only for being too moderate, the Labour Party aligned itself with very many of the Conservative government's propositions by the time of the 1997 general election. Indeed, Labour's general position on sentencing policy, as presented during the passage of the Crime (Sentences) Act 1997, appeared to go further than that of the government.

The entire status of law and order as a party political issue has changed since the 1991 Act was conceived while Douglas Hurd was Home Secretary in Mrs Thatcher's administration. The Major administration won the general election in April 1992, but shortly before the 1991 Act was brought into force in October 1992 the government was permanently destabilised by the country's enforced departure from the European Exchange Rate Mechanism. It was also a time when there was a peak in the figures of recorded crime.

The first repudiation of parts of the Act took place in an atmosphere of media hyperbole on crime, largely conditioned by the tragic case of the toddler, James Bulger, who was murdered by two 10-year-olds. In response to Tony Blair's commitment to be 'tough on crime and tough on the causes of crime' John Major instituted a 'crusade against crime' and called for more condemnation of criminals. Several newspapers maintained a concerted campaign to assert that the criminal justice system was too soft, and neither the then government nor the opposition gave any sign of thinking differently.

The courts reacted quickly to all this, so that by the time of the 1997 general election the use of imprisonment was higher than it had been for 50 years. At the time of the 1992 general election the prison population was about 45,000 and falling; by the time of the 1997 general election it was at the record figure of about 60,000 and growing fast. By the end of 1997 the figure was over 63,500, and still rising. We explain in chapter 2 why increased imprisonment has only a marginal effect on the amount of crime, which is more effectively tackled in other ways. The vital fact that seems to have been sidelined in public awareness is that the number of people convicted of more serious (i.e., indictable) offences has fallen by 10 per cent since 1991.

There is a real danger that, under political encouragement for harsh sentencing that is totally unprecedented in modern times, this country is slipping into ever-greater reliance on the use of imprisonment, at an escalating and underestimated resource cost, with serious consequences for the prison system, with at best only marginal improvement in public protection in the short term and with a real prospect of reduced public protection in the longer term. To our mind, exactly the wrong lessons seem to have been learnt from the USA, where the violent crime rate and other circumstances are very different from our own.

At present this country seems to be moving away from Western European norms for the use of imprisonment, towards a level above that of several of the former Soviet bloc countries. Even the proponents of the policy must admit that its effectiveness against crime is not supported by the great weight of thinking and research about these issues over the years, so that it must at best be seen as a great gamble. Alternatively, it can only be rationalised in terms of pure retribution — that there is something about this country that requires substantially more punishment than do other Western European countries in order to ensure political stability. There is certainly every reason to believe that once heavy retribution becomes accepted by politicians and the public it is extraordinarily hard to reverse the trend. Nevertheless, we believe that sooner or later the need to stablise the situation will become inescapable.

This book shows how earlier attempts to establish a better ordered linkage between sentencing and prison capacity have foundered, and how mistakes have been made on all sides. In particular, the last few years have seen unprecedented denigration of the courts, coupled with an equally unprecedented rise in the weight of the sentences they have passed. That cannot be the foundation for a sensible way forward, but the increased weight of sentencing now seems deeply entrenched.

If there is to be a change of course on the present high imprisonment policy, one vital requirement will be to demystify the subject as much as possible and to put far more effort into explaining the real facts of crime control to the public. Beyond that, the basic issue of the judiciary's relation to the rest of the criminal justice system will surely have to be revisited yet again and it is important that lessons are learned from all that has happened in the last 20 years. As we write, the government appears to be simultaneously offering reassurance that its pre-election position on the use of custody remains unchanged, while recognising that new terms of intervention are required, especially among young people. The jury is still out on where the use of custody is really heading. We believe the situation can only be significantly influenced by very overt political leadership.

In the longer term it may come to be seen that a vital turning point was marked by the government's proposals for new duties to be placed on the Court of Appeal. It may just be that these do provide the basis for a more stable future. In one vital area, however, the court's proposed duties appear too limited. We explain in chapter 11 why we believe the time has come to establish a linkage — however generalised — between sentencing and the capacity of the penal system.

Part 1 of this book sets out the main background issues; Part 2 describes in some detail the most important policy interventions in the 1980s and 1990s; Part 3 summarises where we stand today and what the prospects are for the future.

PART 1

BACKGROUND ISSUES

2 Justifications and Purposes of Imprisonment

Nobody asks why we need schools or hospitals, or what their functions are supposed to be. Prisons, however, are something else again. There are not many important jobs where the entire rationale of the work is, rightly, under such recurrent scrutiny, and someone going to work in the prison service for the first time will feel this quite acutely. Before one can say anything much about prison issues it is necessary to address the basic questions and at least indicate the purposes that imprisonment is supposed to fulfil. What follows is a very compressed account of the propositions that are conventionally cited, but we think that the considerations that should govern rational policy-making on this subject do boil down to a few essential issues, and we believe that what follows is a fair summary.

There is a distinction between seeing punishment as the way in which a society expresses blame, and seeing it as a way to secure particular objectives (always the reduction of crime) by changing offenders' behaviour or circumscribing their freedom of action. There are various sub-plots within these major themes — such as the argument that a credible system of State punishment is required to divert victimised individuals from feeling the need to exact their own vengeance. In an influential book[1] H.L.A. Hart drew a distinction between the 'general justifying aims' for having a system of punishment and the principles of distribution that should determine how punishment is allocated to individual offenders. Hart argued that the general

---

[1] Hart, H.L.A., *Punishment and Responsibility* (Oxford: Clarendon Press, 1968).

aim is the prevention and control of crime, while individual distribution should be according to the principle of desert.

In practice, there is a consensus that the main justifications for punishment boil down to the following four aspects:

(a)   deterrence (both 'specific' to the individual offender and 'general' to exert a deterrent influence on the population at large);

(b)   rehabilitation (to reform the offender's character, rather than frightening him into good future behaviour);

(c)   incapacitation (preventing the offender from committing crimes in society — normally by locking him up, though banishment and capital punishment are also incapacitating penalties to which we shall make no further reference);

(d)   retribution (making offenders suffer punishment because they deserve it).

It is obvious that the first three of these concepts are forward-looking, with the aim of reducing crime, and that it is therefore possible to make a meaningful effort to estimate their success in meeting that aim. There is, in fact, a large research literature by people who have tried to measure the effect of punishment on offenders' behaviour.

Retribution, however, is free-standing and not susceptible to empirical testing, except that a punishment system justified on retributive grounds should be internally proportionate and coherent, so that self-evidently lesser offences do not receive greater punishment than more serious ones and vice versa. It is, however, just as possible to have a coherent and moderate punishment system as a coherent and severe one. The overall severity of a punishment system is rooted deep in a society's culture.

In addition to the classic justifications of punishment set out above there is the alternative approach that offenders should compensate their victims and/or wider society for the wrong they have done. That principle is represented in our law by compensation orders, which require the offender to make a payment to the victim or the victim's relatives, and which courts have to consider ordering in every case involving death, injury, loss or damage. Community service orders are a way of punishing an offender by making him do useful work for the community as a whole. At the present time a debate is developing on restorative justice, which seeks to move away from the conventional analysis we have described here, and into new areas of mediation and involvement of victims and offenders. This approach offers new ways of making offenders face up to their crimes, and it is potentially a very hopeful development. The government's proposal for a new kind of reparation order for young offenders is very welcome, though the subject goes far beyond the scope of this book.

The penalty of imprisonment, by its nature, spreads across the categories of justification in a way that other forms of punishment do not. An offender who is given a prison sentence that is primarily chosen on grounds of retribution will inevitably also be incapacitated from committing offences (outside prison, at least) during the duration of his sentence; an optimist might hope that the prison experience would reform him; and a disciplinarian might believe that the experience and knowledge of the punishment would act as a deterrent to the offender and/or others.

This pooling and blurring of the aims of imprisonment — involving ideas both of punishment and crime control — makes the subject extremely hard to explain to the public, though better public understanding is essential. Most of the public probably see the two things as so closely connected as to be identical. In fact, the fit between the two is a very imperfect one, as we shall try to summarise.

The confusion of rationales has always bedevilled the pursuit of a rational sentencing and imprisonment policy. It has in the past meant that policy-makers have slid from one rationale to another as empirical analysis has undermined previous justifications; it still means that politicians can lump together different justifications in a way that confuses serious analysis; and it has been one of the factors that have enabled sentencers to adopt what has been called a 'cafeteria' approach from a menu of competing rationales to find the justification that most supports their gut feeling about the sentence they sense to be appropriate. One of the main themes of this book is, in fact, that a great increase in the use of imprisonment has been encouraged and planned in the last few years on the ostensible basis that it is a necessary part of an effective crime control strategy, whereas the truth is that it has been an exercise in retribution that has demonstrably had little to do with crime control.

Nevertheless, there is plenty of evidence available on the first three of the possible aims of imprisonment listed above, and in the rest of this chapter we summarise the main points that we think a disinterested adviser should be reporting to policy-makers at the present time.

DETERRENCE

The idea of specific deterrence is that the experience of a punishment is so unpleasant that the offender alters his behaviour to reduce the risk of being punished again. Most offenders on leaving prison would probably say — and indeed believe — that they will try to avoid another unpleasant experience of prison, but the well-known fact is that, when allowance is made for the differences between the groups, reconviction rates are essentially the same for ex-prisoners as for those given various kinds of non-custodial sentences.[2] There are doubtless prisoners who are deterred by their experience of prison, just as there are probationers who are deterred by their experience of probation, but imprisonment, as such, does not appear to be an especially effective type of sentence from the point of view of deterring subsequent criminal behaviour by those who experience it. Attempts have been made in this country and others to subject prisoners to regimes that are so unpleasant that they exert a special deterrent effect, but these appear to be a blind alley. Thus, the 'short, sharp shock' detention centre regime that was experimentally established in the early 1980s following the 1979 Conservative election manifesto proved to have no better post-release reconviction scores than centres operating the normal regime. Whether the last Conservative government's experimental 'boot camp' regime should be seen as primarily deterrent or reformative in intention is a nice question, since it was presented as a cocktail of both principles, as were some of its exemplars in the USA. Certainly, American 'boot camp' regimes of the aggressive kind have not been shown to be at all effective in discouraging reoffending.

If punitive regimes are not the answer, though, surely longer sentences must have a potent effect in deterring the individual from reoffending? Once again, the research literature indicates otherwise. While there is some evidence that the prospect of long sentences is among the factors that weigh with mature recidivists who decide to give up a life of crime, this seems to be part of a general ageing development, and the evidence does not support the idea that long sentences in themselves are generally effective deterrents to those who experience them.

The question of general deterrence is, perhaps, more complex. First of all, there is empirical evidence that the very existence of a system of law enforcement does have a general deterrent effect on crime, just as one would expect. The classic case that is quoted is the removal for some months of the Danish police force by the occupying Germans in the Second World War, and the subsequent vivid rise in offences of theft and robbery.

The question that is relevant to policy-making, however, is the relationship between increases of penalty levels and the incidence of the relevant offending behaviour, and here there appears to be simply no sufficient evidence of linkage to support deterrence-based arguments for increasing penalties for particular offences. (There may, of course, be perfectly good reasons for such adjustments on other grounds.) Beyleveld's comprehensive

---

[2] Lloyd, C., Mair, G. and Hough, M., *Explaining Reconviction Rates: a Critical Analysis* (Home Office Research Study No. 136) (London: HMSO, 1994); Kershaw, C., 'Reconvictions of those commencing community penalties in 1993, England and Wales', *Home Office Statistical Bulletin* 6/97 (London: Home Office, 1997).

study in 1980[3] brought out very clearly the extreme rarity of instances in which changes in levels of offending could confidently be attributed to fear of a particular penalty as opposed to other considerations. It also stressed that the key factor in deterrence is not the objectively demonstrable risk of punishment but the individual potential offender's perception of the risk of being caught, about which it is extremely unsound to generalise from the basis of one's personal experience. This is not to say that deterrent effects are never obtainable, but simply that there is no reliable basis for assuming them. There is, for example, some evidence, such as Harding's study of Canadian robbers' attitudes towards carrying firearms,[4] that offenders of particular categories who are prone to plan ahead may tend to be influenced by special penalties. On the other hand — and this is particularly relevant to current political argument — there is specific research[5] on burglars that shows them to be predominantly feckless people with a short-term focus, who put out of their minds while committing a crime the possibility of being detected. According to this research, they see themselves as having little choice but to commit burglaries as the only way they know in which to relieve overwhelming immediate needs (usually for money, but sometimes also for self-esteem).

The behavioural psychologists' views on deterrence theory chime in with the above, and boil down to the following.

First, most people have internalised moral scruples about offending. Those who do not have such scruples are deterred much more by informal social control mechanisms such as the opinion of their friends, neighbours and family than by the threat of formal sanctions.[6] As for those who are not inhibited by their own code of values or by informal social control mechanisms, punishment may indeed be an effective agent of change, but only if it scores highly on the following long-recognised features.

(a)   Certainty. Punishment should be the inevitable and unavoidable consequence of the offending behaviour.

(b)   Immediacy. Punishment should follow the offending behaviour rapidly, so as to impress the connection upon the individual.

(c)   Severity. If punishment is not applied with great intensity, its effects are uncertain.

(d)   Comprehensibility. The reason and justification for the punishment should be understood by the individual on whom it is inflicted.

---

[3] Beyleveld, D., *A Bibliography on General Deterrence Research* (Westmead: Saxon House, 1980).

[4] Harding, R., 'Rational choice gun use in armed robbery', 1 *Criminal Law Forum* 427 (1990).

[5] Bennett, T. and Wright, R.T., *Burglars on Burglary* (Aldershot: Gower, 1984); Wright, R.T. and Decker, S.H., *Burglars on the Job* (Boston: North Western University Press, 1994).

[6] Willcock, H.D. and Stokes, J., *Deterrents and Incentives to Crime among Boys and Young Men Aged 15–21 Years* (London: HMSO, 1968).

In addition, James McGuire, whose *What Works*[7] summarises the research evidence, argues that a further necessary criterion is the availability to the individual of alternative means for the achievement of the goals otherwise sought through offending behaviour.

It is immediately obvious how enormously far all these requirements are from the daily reality of the criminal justice processes. Above all, with police clear-up rates at around 25 per cent and with less than 3 per cent of the crimes that are actually committed leading to formal caution or prosecution, the likelihood of punishment for much crime is a very long way from being a certainty. The great criminologist Beccaria is still generally thought to have been absolutely right in his maxim that certainty, rather than severity, is the test of an effective antidote for crime.

Looking beyond the paramount requirement of certainty, the current realities do not score well on the other characteristics of an effective deterrent punishment system. As the Labour government has recognised in respect of youth crime, the delays that have become endemic in our criminal justice mean that the commission of an offence and any eventual punishment for it are widely separated in time. As for severity, we shall be arguing that imprisonment is indeed a harsher sanction than it has recently been fashionable to acknowledge, but many people who go to prison already have very damaged lives, and their perception of risking imprisonment has to be seen in that context.

The conclusion of all this must be that there is no sound evidence for believing that, in the real world, changes in sentencing policy should have any appreciable general deterrent effect on the incidence of crime. If immediate execution was the penalty that was routinely enforced for parking offences then we would no doubt be more careful where we left our cars, but that is a fantasy situation and not a real-world one.

REHABILITATION

The idea of imprisonment having a beneficial reformative effect in itself has had an extraordinarily long history. When modern-style imprisonment took shape at the turn of the eighteenth and nineteenth centuries as a replacement for earlier corporal punishment systems, the dominant theme was one of enforced monastic isolation in which the offender should contemplate his sins and his need for redemption. The very words 'penitentiary', 'reformatory', 'corrections' say as much — as well as reminding us how much of our penal thinking in this country has been influenced by agendas set in the USA, by no means always to our advantage.

---

[7] McGuire, J. (ed.), *What Works: Reducing Reoffending* (Chichester: Wiley, 1995).

Throughout the nineteenth century the rhetoric of reformation coexisted with the harshest penal regimes, and it comes as an astonishing breath of fresh air to read the following reply by Sir Godfrey Lushington, the Permanent Secretary (i.e., the head civil servant) of the Home Office in evidence to the reforming Gladstone Committee in 1895:

I regard as unfavourable to reformation the status of a prisoner throughout his whole career; the crushing of self-respect, the starving of all moral instinct he may possess, the absence of opportunity to do or receive a kindness, the continual association with none but criminals . . . the forced labour and the denial of all liberty. I believe the true mode of reforming a man or restoring him to society is exactly in the opposite direction to all these. But of course this is a mere idea. It is quite impracticable in a prison. In fact, the unfavourable features I have mentioned are inseparable from a prison life. All that I care to insist on is that this treatment is not reformatory. I consider that a mediaeval thief who had his right hand chopped off was much more likely to turn over a new leaf than a convict who has had 10 years penal servitude.[8]

That critique was levelled against a system of prison treatment that now appears unbearably cruel, rigid and coercive. In the event, the Gladstone Committee set deterrence and reformation as the simultaneous aims of imprisonment, and the new emphasis on reformation did lead to a change for the better in the prison system. Yet even today anyone who really knows about prisons must still read Lushington's words with the deeply uncomfortable recognition that much of what he had to say is inherently true of imprisonment by its very nature.

In the twentieth century the reformative ideal reinvented itself in terms of behavioural science rather than religious imperatives and Victorian paternalism. It reached its high point in the 'medical' or 'treatment' model that was widely accepted in the USA in the 1960s, before spectacularly crashing in the 1970s. What then brought it down was the combined onslaught of empirical analysts who demonstrated that exposure to prison regimes of whatever duration did not of itself have a reformative effect in terms of reconviction rates, and civil libertarians who demonstrated that the indeterminate sentencing that went with the treatment model led to capricious post-sentence decision-making, including inbuilt bias against ethnic and other groups. What is nowadays virtually universally accepted is that imprisonment of itself does not have a reformative effect, but that certain kinds of treatment programme can have a significant effect in reducing

---

[8] Evidence to Home Office Departmental Committee on Prisons 1895, Q.11482.

offending behaviour among certain groups of individuals, and that pro-grammes of these kinds can be administered in prison.

The current state of the art in this area is conveniently summarised by James McGuire in *What Works*.[9] McGuire argues that, while more research is needed, the technique of meta analysis (which involves aggregating and re-analysing the results of different research projects) has clearly indicated the general characteristics of treatment programmes that are successful. The statistical level of success, measured against control groups, is claimed to be of the order of 10 per cent, with treatment programmes in the community being about twice as effective as those within penal institutions. Successful programmes are focused on the factors that caused individuals to offend, and those that employ cognitive behavioural methodology are found to work best. Effective programmes rely on clear aims and explicitly defined methods; they require well-trained and properly resourced staff; and it is essential that the objectives underpinning the work should be adhered to (i.e., the programme should deliver what has been undertaken to the participants). There needs to be managerial support, a commitment to evaluation, and mechanisms for feeding the results of evaluation back into the conduct of the programme.

People involved with prisons have often been tempted in the past to claim more for their rehabilitative role than the system can actually deliver. Claims of that sort make their originators feel better about the machine with which they are involved and they are very understandable. Nevertheless, they blur a clear focus on the nature of imprisonment, and they have sometimes led to mistaken policies. Modern offending behaviour programmes are one of the most important developments now going on in the prison world, and their recent establishment throughout the English prison system has been a very positive step. While rehabilitation programmes of this kind are a very necessary and worthwhile thing to pursue within prisons, however, they do not overturn the generally accepted proposition that people should not be sent to prison simply for rehabilitation.

INCAPACITATION

It has always been blindingly clear that, whatever prisons cannot do, the one thing that they can achieve is to keep people locked up so that they cannot commit crimes outside in society. Nevertheless, incapacitation as a general theory of imprisonment has historically been given less attention than deterrence and rehabilitation. It has only been as those justifications for imprisonment have been eroded that the study of incapacitation has moved into the forefront, first in the USA and now in this country.

---

[9] See note 7.

Imprisonment on grounds of incapacitation involves detaining (and, if done in prison, inevitably punishing) people not for what they have done but for what it is thought they might do if they were at liberty. It manifestly involves both the technical issue of prediction and the ethical issue of what degree of predictive certainty is required to justify an individual's continued detention. In practice, elements of incapacitatory thinking have always been likely to be involved in the sentencing of the 'dangerous offender' and the 'persistent offender', though the incapacitation element may well exist alongside and be submerged by other rationales.

The problem with the 'dangerous offender' is that grave violent offences are rare occurrences that are difficult to predict, so that even the best developed methods only reach an accuracy of 50 per cent, with one 'false positive' for each 'true positive'. To the extent that 'dangerous offenders' bring themselves into that category by grave offences in the first place, long sentences will usually be merited on straightforward grounds of proportionality, and it has always been the case that this may mask an element of public protection. Difficult decisions then have to be made, however, in considering the release of a life-sentence prisoner or the early release of a fixed-sentence one, since conduct in prison may be no reliable indication of behaviour on release. The most problematic cases are those of people whose immediate offence is not especially grave, but who give cause for genuine concern about their dangerous propensities. There is, of course, a mental health element in virtually all such cases, and the particular problem of the so-called psychopath (whose behaviour is not normal, but who is generally not treatable and hence within the ambit of restraint authorised on medical grounds) has been an unresolved matter of concern for at least the last 25 years.

The persistent (but not dangerous) offender also will merit a long sentence if his immediate offence is a grave one. The question to which sentencers and politicians have constantly reverted, however, is what to do about persistent non-violent property offenders, who constantly reoffend, but who never commit crimes that are big enough in themselves to justify long imprisonment. One answer is simply to punish them in proportion to what they have done and to accept with resignation that they are quite likely to do something similar again until they give up crime. But if that measure of political and judicial acceptance is jettisoned, the only alternative is specially long confinement for such offenders, which has been the central feature of many failed policies in English penal history. One example from the nineteenth century is the 'cumulative principle' advocated by a Gloucestershire magistrate, Barwick Lloyd Baker, in 1863.[10] This principle required that

---

[10] The cumulative principle arguably combined specific deterrence and incapacitation.

the punishment for a first felony conviction should be a week or so's imprisonment on bread and water, for the second a year's imprisonment, for the third seven years' penal servitude, and for the fourth life imprisonment. With a tone of hermetic certainty that has uncanny echoes of some current political attitudes, Baker calmly asserted that 'if you tell a man clearly what will be the punishment of a crime before he commits it, there can be no injustice in inflicting it', though his approach proved highly controversial and was disowned by the Lord Chief Justice of the day. Later, the Prevention of Crime Act 1908, enabled courts to impose a supplementary sentence of preventive detention, in addition to the current sentence, on convicted felons with three previous felony convictions. Churchill, when Home Secretary, was enraged to find these powers being used against petty pilferers and he issued a circular demanding that the additional sanction should only be invoked against offenders who were 'a serious danger to society'. After that, the use of the power withered away, but it was only to be resuscitated in a different guise by the Criminal Justice Act 1948, which authorised sentences of preventive detention between five and 14 years for persistent offenders. Preventive detainees serving enormous sentences for trivial offences are well within the memory of the present authors (one chronic pilferer comes to mind who, in the early 1960s, was serving 14 years for stealing a chicken). Eventually the judges themselves turned against this sort of thing and the power was repealed, only to be replaced by the extended sentence provisions in the Criminal Justice Act 1967, which never caught on.

What the 'cumulative principle' and the various statutory provisions for preventive confinement do seem to show is, first, that there is nothing new under the sun so far as penal policy is concerned and, second, that institutionalised attempts to protect society from the non-violent persistent offender have always foundered on the inherent tendency of such arrange-ments to suck in less serious offenders, whose disproportionately heavy punishment becomes unacceptable. Alongside the structured policy initiat-ives, however, there exists the informal courtroom practice of 'sentencing on record' (i.e., simply sentencing multiple recidivists more severely than their current offence justifies) and this is harder to pin down, though the practice is probably still alive and well. 'Sentencing on record' was at the bottom of one of the policies in the Criminal Justice Act 1991 that was abruptly reversed in 1993.

Setting aside all considerations of proportionality and fairness, the basic questions faced by incapacitation theory are how to select the offenders to be given the preventive confinement, and how to quantify the crime that is prevented by taking them out of circulation. Since the sole justification of incapacitation policy is to prevent crime, policy-makers taking this path should have an accurate assessment of the amount of crime reduction that is bought by imprisonment programmes that inevitably involve high resource costs (together with less easily quantifiable human costs).

One approach to crime control by incapacitation would simply be greatly to increase sentence lengths across the board, on the proposition that the offending behaviour of many criminals is known to range across a variety of offence categories, and that the more criminals in prison, the less crime would necessarily be committed. A smarter, more cost-effective, approach would be one that tried to exploit the fact that a disproportionate amount of crime is committed by a comparatively small number of high-rate offenders. Such an approach would try to home in on the defining characteristics of the high-rate offenders and put away those people who corresponded to the resulting descriptive profile. If that kind of approach was found not to be workable, one might try to obtain at least some of its benefits by defining a profile of previous offending, which is known to be a very significant indicator of future offending, and giving long preventive sentences to people who clocked up the necessary qualifying convictions. All these approaches have had their proponents in the last few decades and they have, in fact, been given the distinguishing names of collective, selective and categorial incapacitation, respectively.[11]

There is a persuasive feel of simplicity about the idea of dealing with crime by putting the high-rate offender out of action, but in practice the proposition tends to fall apart. This is primarily because crime is something that is done by a surprisingly large part of the population, and most criminal careers are fairly short. No less than 34 per cent of males and 8 per cent of females will have a conviction for a 'standard list' offence[12] before the age of 40 (though more than half of that number will only have been convicted once). Crime is also a young person's game, predominantly being carried out by young males during a comparatively short period in their lives. The peak age for known offending is 18 for males and 14 for females.[13]

Crime is, therefore, not an activity that is mainly conducted by an easily identifiable and finite group of special people called criminals but is, rather, the product of a very large and volatile pool, constantly being both replenished and diminished as individuals move into and out of criminal activity. At no time can one know with certainty how large that pool is, or what is the rate of offending by the individuals within it. Neither can one know what would be the rate of offending by the imprisoned and incapacitated population if it was at liberty, though incarcerated individuals who are

---

[11] See, for example, Von Hirsch, A., *Past or Future Crimes* (Manchester: Manchester University Press, 1986).

[12] The 'standard list' includes all indictable offences and some of the more serious summary ones.

[13] All the figures in this paragraph are taken from Barclay, G.C., Tavares, C. and Prout, A., *Information on the Criminal Justice System in England and Wales* (London: Home Office, 1995).

well advanced in their criminal careers (as many will tend to be if they have had time to clock up qualifying convictions) must be expected to reduce and desist from offending under the normal process of maturation and settling down. Two highly relevant considerations are the fact that many offences are carried out as joint enterprises, so that the incapacitation of one individual will not necessarily have much effect on offence rates if his criminal colleagues remain active, and the fact that some criminal activities (drug dealing is the example that is usually given) reflect market principles, so that the place of one incapacitated supplier is likely to be promptly taken by a new recruit. Additionally, all prison populations are already skewed towards persistent and high-rate offenders, so any expansion of them is bound to represent diminishing margins of improvement in crime prevention.

The distinguished criminologists Franklin Zimring and Gordon Hawkins, in their respected book *Incapacitation*,[14] warn against attempting to make global estimates of the amount of crime prevention that is obtainable by incapacitation, saying 'the amount of crime prevented by incapacitation is both variable and contingent, varying in relation to different social circumstances and under different criminal justice policies'. That is a wise health warning, especially in the context of the USA, where so many different criminal justice systems and policies operate simultaneously at federal and state level. In the context of a single jurisdiction such as England and Wales we believe that it is possible to arrive at a meaningful estimate of the incapacitatory effect, as an essential aid to policy-makers. So far as we are aware, the fullest examination in the United Kingdom of the crime-reduction effects of incapacitation remains the work published in 1993[15] by Roger Tarling, then head of the Home Office Research and Planning Unit. Tarling concluded that there was little ground for thinking that sentences could efficiently be targeted on groups that were particularly likely to reoffend, and his key conclusion was that 'a change in the use of custody of the order of 25 per cent would be needed to produce a 1 per cent change in the level of crime'. In other words, doubling the prison population would reduce crime by just 4 per cent, which is a figure that is well within the fluctuations of the rate at which people report crimes to the police and the rate at which the police record the crimes that are reported to them.

One of the unsatisfactory features of the Parliamentary discussion of the Crime (Sentences) Act 1997 was the slight attention that was given to exploring the crime-reduction effect of those very costly proposals, though Tarling's findings were mentioned by some critics of the legislation. We have absolutely no reason to suppose that further research would come to conclusions very different from Tarling's or that his 25-to-one gearing

---

[14] Zimring, F. and Hawkins, G., *Incapacitation* (New York: Oxford University Press, 1995).

[15] Tarling, R., *Analysing Offending: Data, Models and Interpretations* (London: HMSO 1993).

between the crime rate and the size of the prison population would be moved into a different ballpark. We believe that this is the line that a disinterested adviser should be putting to policy-makers at the present time. Nevertheless, as part of the rationalisation and demystification that is so much needed, it would be desirable for the government to consider if further research could establish more facts about rates and patterns of offending.

The gearing that we have indicated between prison populations and crime rates, together with the high resource costs of imprisonment, means that expanding the prison population of a country that already has a high rate of imprisonment is inherently unlikely to represent a very effective way of responding to crime. Nevertheless, when incapacitation is presented as the only option it has a simplicity and clarity of aim that gives it great political potency. Zimring and Hawkins put this perfectly in *Incapacitation* when they wrote:

> Just as locking up more offenders *must* reduce criminal activity by some amount, releasing large numbers of offenders or allowing them to remain outside prison *must* produce some increase in the number of crimes experienced by the community that receives them. Support of decarceration is thus the moral equivalent of approving higher crime rates, entailing a high risk of political extinction for anyone sufficiently naive to endorse the policy.

We would only add that the fear of political extinction seems now to extend well beyond the topic of reducing prison numbers: it would be more accurate to say that it inhibits any questioning of the need to go on increasing the scale of imprisonment.

CONCLUSIONS

The purpose of this chapter has simply been to establish the starting point by setting out what we believe to be the current views among mainstream informed opinion in this country about the purposes of imprisonment and about its effectiveness in those aspects that are, in principle, measurable.

It is perfectly true to say that the existence of the prison sanction is a deterrent, but there is no sound basis for claiming much for the deterrent effects of sentencing changes. Some kinds of rehabilitation programmes in prison have some effect with some kinds of offenders (though less successfully than in a non-penal setting) but offenders should not be sent to prison simply for rehabilitation. As for incapacitation, nobody doubts the need to protect the public from genuinely dangerous offenders (with all the issues of identification, procedural justice and risk assessment that this involves), but enormous numbers of people would theoretically have to be imprisoned to have an appreciable effect on the general crime rate.

All this kind of crime control argument can very easily turn out to be irrelevant since the political decision-maker can always claim to be articulating what is 'right' by way of retribution pure and simple, and then the need for more punishment is likely to be put to the public as something that is self-evident.

Punishment has a powerful symbolic function. Inflicting punishment has always been one of the main ways in which a State projects itself as powerful and effective (and the less confident a government is, the more need it probably sees for such props). These aspects are similar to the theme of nationalism in foreign policy. People do need to feel that they are properly protected and that criminals are punished, just as they need to feel that the government is protecting national interests. If the public are constantly told that punishment is inadequate and that much more of it is easily available, then of course they will want to see it delivered. Once confidence is undermined and the genie of punishment as the answer to crime is let out of the bottle, it is extraordinarily difficult — perhaps impossible — to get it back in again.

3   Prisons since the 1970s

This chapter simply summarises the main developments of the last couple of decades in order to put the present scale of imprisonment into perspective.

The first point to stress is that the prison system's tasks and security requirements interact in quite a complex way that tends to make the system inflexible. Remand prisoners[1] should be accommodated separately from sentenced ones; young offenders separately from adults; women separately from men. Since 1966 there has been a security classification system which divides sentenced prisoners into four categories, with category A for the most serious security risks, for whom escape has to be made as difficult as possible, and category D for prisoners who present a minimum risk to the public and who can go to open prisons. Categories B and C are for intermediate levels of security and all unsentenced prisoners are regarded as being category B except for a few provisionally categorised A. The security of any given establishment is largely dependant upon its architecture and hardware (e.g., high perimeter walls and closed-circuit television surveillance) and partly upon its operating regime (e.g., frequency of searching, amount of specialist staff time given to security work). Establishments (and, in some cases, parts of establishments) are graded into the four security categories and no prisoners should be held in conditions that have a lower security grading than their own categorisation.

There are two main kinds of prison establishment. Local prisons hold both remand prisoners and prisoners serving short sentences, and they keep newly sentenced prisoners long enough to categorise them and allocate them to

---

[1] We will use the expression 'remand prisoners' to include all unsentenced prisoners, though there are technical differences within the group.

other prisons. There are a few remand centres that carry out these functions for young offenders. The other main kind of establishment consists of training prisons and young offender institutions, which hold sentenced prisoners serving longer sentences. Although the main types of prison are clear enough, in practice there is nowadays a great deal of mixed use, so that a training prison for adult males may have a section for young offenders, or for remand prisoners, or for women.

Running the prison system therefore requires a constant juggling act to match the types of establishment with the profile of the prison population and to get the right prisoners in the right places at the right time. Remand prisoners ought to be close to the courts and lawyers dealing with their cases; all prisoners need to be kept at a level of security that is adequate for them; long-sentence prisoners should have the opportunity of following some meaningful kind of training and prison career plan; young offenders (especially children) should be kept apart from adults, men away from women. On top of that, all prisoners should be as close as practicable to their homes since one of the few things that is agreed by everybody in the prison world is the importance of prisoners maintaining contact with their families. The Woolf report (of which more later) recommended in 1991 that the idea of 'community prisons' should be developed, so that prisoners of various categories could be held in an establishment, or cluster of establishments, near to their homes. The great problem with mixing very different categories in the same prison is that the requirements of the different groups are markedly diverse and need different handling. It has always been accepted, for example, that young offenders should be kept separate from experienced recidivist adult offenders, and that their educational and training needs are quite different from those of adults. This means that the training and experience of staff also need to be different. In practice, the staff culture of individual prisons is very deeply rooted and there are great differences in staff attitudes not only between the different classes of prisons, but also between different prisons of the same class. Forming geographical clusters of prisons with different functions is the more practical way of implementing Woolf's humane and sensible proposal, but that sort of rational planning is exactly the sort of thing that is impossible when the whole system is overloaded by excessive numbers of prisoners.

During the late 1970s and 1980s the prison system was quite clearly going through a long series of serious crises of different kinds, and it is extremely depressing to recall it. Its professed aspiration remained an idealistic mission of industry and reform, as articulated in the system of training prisons for adult prisoners, and a considerable amount of new industrial plant had, in fact, been put in place during the 1970s. In reality, however, there had been an almost complete loss of confidence in rehabilitation, and the prison service was stumbling around unsuccessfully in a search for something to fill the vacuum. In the absence of anything else, sheer custodianship and security came close to appearing to be what it was all about.

Alongside this confusion and sterility of rationale several extremely negative aspects were unfolding simultaneously and feeding from each other. In the first place, there was a relentless increase in the level of overcrowding. Not much new prison building had been commissioned since the Second World War and the increasing numbers sent from the courts posed a severe problem. The government responded in two ways. First, as we discuss in chapter 7, it took action in 1984 and 1987 to increase the amount of parole and remission for short-sentence prisoners so that they served less of their sentences in prison. Second, a large building programme was set in train in 1982 and subsequently expanded so that 21 new prisons were in use by 1994. In the meantime overcrowding steadily got worse through the 1980s. The conventional way of measuring overcrowding is by reference to the 'certified normal accommodation' (CNA) of each establishment, which is supposed to represent the full but not crowded capacity. There are arguments about the reliability of the CNA but it is a broadly adequate guide and there is no alternative on offer. During the 1970s the population was running at an average of 8.5 per cent over CNA and this rose to between 10 and 15 per cent throughout the 1980s with a peak of about 22 per cent in 1987.

The second important factor was the astonishingly poor state of industrial relations in the prison service. There were many reasons for this, including the perceived remoteness of the central management structure, the climate of public-sector union militancy in the 1970s, the poor working conditions of the staff and the introduction of specialists of various kinds, which was seen by uniformed prison officers as limiting their role to that of turnkeys. Whatever one's view of all the causes, the authority of managers at every level of the prison service was precariously balanced and the prison officers, acting through the Prison Officers Association (POA), constantly used industrial action to further their demands. It was inherent in the situation that the people who inevitably lost out from industrial action were the prisoners, whose welfare therefore became a bargaining counter between staff and managers. All this was made yet worse by pay structures that actively encouraged staff to work overtime, so there was an inbuilt pressure for lists of agreed tasks to be inflated under dire warnings of the likely consequences to security if the staff's assessments were not accepted.

It was the state of industrial relations that was the main reason for the appointment of the Committee of Inquiry under Lord Justice May in 1978. The May Committee's report in 1979[2] agreed that 'the rhetoric of treatment and training has had its day' but could not bring itself to agree with reasoned

---

[2] Committee of Inquiry into the United Kingdom Prison Services, *Report* (Cmnd 7673) (London: HMSO, 1979).

evidence from Roy King and Rod Morgan that imprisonment should recognise the principles of minimum use of custody, minimum use of security, and normalisation. Instead, the May Committee argued in favour of a rather vague idea of 'positive custody' and made some proposals about management organisation and pay and conditions of staff that were an insufficient basis for real lasting change. By 1980 the POA was taking industrial action on a national scale and there had to be emergency legislation — the Imprisonment (Temporary Provisions) Act 1980 — to reduce the frequency with which remand prisoners had to be taken to court, and to take cover for the prison service in various other ways.

The upshot of all these factors was plain enough to anybody who saw much of prisons in the early 1980s. Overcrowding was concentrated in the local prisons, where there was often little pretence of any activity for the prisoners, many of whom were locked up two or three to a cell for 23 hours a day. In the majority of locals these conditions were made disgraceful by the sanitary arrangements, which took the form of plastic pots, which the prisoners were let out to empty at infrequent intervals in the degrading ritual of 'slopping out'. Every day there was a great exodus of staff from the locals to accompany the prisoners to court, and every evening in many parts of the country there was a horse-trading session with the local police whereby several hundred prisoners who could not be squeezed into prisons were parked in police cells, sometimes for weeks at a time. At times the cells at local courts were also used for accommodating surplus prisoners.

Prison service management did not pursue a deliberate policy of trying to spread the overcrowding more evenly through the whole system, and it has been strongly criticised for this on the cogent argument that it left the untried prisoners who enjoyed the presumption of innocence to put up with the most indefensible conditions. The arguments were not all one way. Amongst other considerations, making long-term prisoners share their cells could have sparked off control problems, about which the prison service had very good reason to be apprehensive at the time.

In the training prisons conditions were not overcrowded as they were in the locals, and the prisoners in them spent much more time out of their cells. That does not mean that all was well in the training prisons. In reality it was quite evident that the number of staff in proportion to the prisoners had swollen enormously, while the amount of work and other worthwhile activity that was being offered to the prisoners had steadily shrunk.[3] On top of this litany of ills, the prison system was prone to intermittent riots in the training prisons, and especially in the small number of high-security 'dispersal'

---

[3] The increase in staff and deterioration of regimes is documented in King, R.D. and McDermott, K., 'British prisons 1970–1987: the ever-deepening crisis', *British Journal of Criminology*, vol. 29 pp. 107–28 (1989).

prisons in which category A prisoners were held along with larger numbers of long-term prisoners of lower security categories.

During the 1980s disturbances spread to other kinds of establishment including, in April 1986, a spectacular wave of rioting at 40 prisons, sparked off by prison officers refusing to work overtime in protest at staffing levels in local prisons and remand centres. Eventually, in April and May 1990 an extremely severe and prolonged riot at Strangeways Prison, Manchester, sparked off another bout of rioting in other establishments and Lord Justice Woolf (now Lord Woolf and Master of the Rolls) was appointed, together with the Chief Inspector of Prisons, Judge Tumim, to hold yet another committee of inquiry.[4] Strangeways was a local prison and it had become quite impossible to see the control problem as something special to the high-security prisons for long term prisoners. Clearly something much deeper was involved, and the massive Woolf report,[5] published in February 1991, rose to the occasion by setting out the most fundamental analysis and forward-looking agenda since the Gladstone Committee in 1895. Woolf's report was, in fact, a far more impressive document than Gladstone's and we believe that its core proposals do set out the way in which a decent and effective prison system should be run.

Woolf concentrated on what imprisonment was actually like. The report is permeated by the diagnosis that the system depended on the right balance between the requirements of security, control and justice, and that in addition to the evident failure of control there had been a failure to provide an acceptable standard of justice. His concept of justice was as wide as the word can bear, and this enabled him to bring together a range of aims that he believed the prison service must be assumed to have undertaken in further-ance of the just sentence or order of the court. Thus, although he was careful to distance himself from the 'treatment model', Woolf argued that a sentence of imprisonment must be held to imply a positive approach to looking after prisoners with humanity, safeguarding prisoners' civil rights, minimising the negative aspects of imprisonment and providing prisoners with the opportun-ity to obtain skills. None of this was new, but it had never been assembled so powerfully or articulated in such a coherent reform programme.

The central concern with justice underlies the report's specific proposals for better grievance procedures, major changes to the disciplinary system,[6] and a completely new statement of purpose for remand prisoners. It was also the basis for wider recommendations for prisoners to be given reasons for

[4] The appointment of an independent inspector of prisons had been recommended by the May committee.

[5] Woolf, Lord Justice and Tumim, Judge Stephen, *Prison Disturbances April 1990: Report of an Inquiry* (Cm 1456) (London: HMSO, 1991).

[6] Including, most importantly, the abolition of disciplinary proceedings by prison boards of visitors.

decisions, for the progressive establishment of prison standards and for 'compacts' with prisoners that would spell out their expectations and responsibilities. In order to maintain family ties telephones should be made available to prisoners, the entitlement to visits should be increased and prisons should be planned and grouped so that most prisoners could be kept near their homes. The idea of 'compacts' was followed through in recommendations for the Director General to have a visible leadership role under a contract with ministers, and for a great deal of responsibility to be delegated from the centre to governors of establishments and their staff. On the most glaring evil of prison life, Woolf recommended that all prisoners should have access to sanitation by February 1996. Woolf's terms of reference kept him away from sentencing policy, but his proposal of a Criminal Justice Consultative Council came as close as he could to suggesting that the ideas of criminal justice and of planning were not mutually contradictory. The council was to be a national body with local committees that would involve the judiciary and the other main players with the object of developing closer cooperation. Woolf did not believe that there was a single cause for what had gone wrong in the prisons, but he had no doubt that overcrowding was one of the most important background factors. He recommended that there should be a new provision in the Prison Rules that no prison should hold more than 3 per cent above its CNA, with provision for Parliament to be informed if the rule was breached. He hoped that overcrowding could be 'outlawed' by 1992.

The last recommendation was rejected outright by the government, and the recommendation for a Criminal Justice Consultative Council initially ran into problems with the then Lord Chief Justice, Lord Lane, who thought that the judiciary's participation would jeopardise their independence. That obstacle was removed by Lord Taylor of Gosforth when he succeeded Lane. For the rest, the Home Secretary, Kenneth Baker, showed real commitment to prison reform by generally accepting the Woolf agenda in the White Paper, *Custody, Care and Justice*,[7] though nothing much was promised on overcrowding and no firm timescale was offered on most of the recommendations. On the other hand, the changes to disciplinary and grievance procedures were put in hand straightaway, most of Woolf's proposals for improving family communication and visits were adopted, and plans were made to end slopping out even earlier than Woolf had proposed. In the event, all prisoners had access to proper sanitation by April 1996.

The Woolf Report came during a time when the prison population was steadily falling from its August 1988 peak of 51,000 to a transient low figure of 40,600 in December 1992. Even when the population began climbing

---

[7] Home Office, *Custody, Care and Justice: the Way Ahead for the Prison Service in England and Wales* (Cmnd 1647) (London: HMSO, 1991).

again in 1993 it was more than offset by the new prison places coming on stream from the 1982 building programme, so that 1993 was the one year since the 1950s when accommodation measured by CNA has been greater than the population. We shall be arguing in chapter 11 that it was that fact that enabled the Conservative government to begin the encouragement of harsher sentencing that still dominates the prison scene.

Relieved of immediate concerns about overcrowding, the prison service was engaged in reinventing itself as a 'Next Steps' agency. Baker's successor as Home Secretary, Kenneth Clarke, took the decision to go for agency status in 1992 and appointed Derek Lewis, a television executive, to take over as Director General when the changeover took place in April 1993. Agencies of this kind were the government's standard model for removing executive areas of work from ministers' immediate suspension within a department, and setting them up under a chief executive responsible for meeting the performance requirements that were periodically negotiated. Agency status was precisely in line with the kind of structural changes that Woolf had advocated, and there was a widespread view in prison reform circles that the greater independence and visibility that were supposed to flow from the status would enable the prison service to win more public understanding.

Agency status is absolutely fine for undertakings that do not attract much political interest, but the more politically interesting the area of work, the greater the difficulties in purporting to respect a separation of policy and operational functions all contained within a minister's ultimate responsibility. Like marriage, it will probably work if both partners are prepared to compromise, but otherwise it is likely to be a rather miserable experience. Whatever views one has about the suitability of agency status for something as politically lively as the prison system, there is no doubt that the business of preparing an organisation for agency status is an extremely demanding exercise in self-examination. It requires activities to be identified, costed and tested with a rigour that can only be beneficial, and which was certainly not amiss in the case of the prison system. Part of the problem in the early 1980s had been the lack of any but the most rudimentary systems for finding out what was actually happening in any given establishment, let alone what cost should be attached to it. A very great deal of work was already being put into this during the 1980s as a result of the government's financial management initiative, which required public-sector bodies to identify their objectives, cost their activities and devolve the control of resources to the management level that had the matching responsibility. The transition to agency status took all these processes a stage further and moved much closer to enabling managers and staff at all levels to be held accountable for the delivery of specified objectives.

In 1987, well before the Woolf Report, the terms and conditions of employment of prison staff had been changed under the fresh start initiative.

This amounted to buying out the prison officers from the old overtime-intensive arrangements and establishing them on a fixed working week. There were severe teething troubles, including staff protest that required the police to be drafted into Wandsworth Prison in 1989, but the change had to be made, as excessive reliance on overtime had come close to making prisons unmanageable.

Alongside the movement to agency status the biggest organisational change in the prison world in the 1990s has been the involvement of the private-sector security industry in the prison system. As late as 1987 Douglas Hurd had said in the House of Commons, 'I do not believe that the House would accept a case for . . . handing over the business of keeping prisoners safe to anyone other than government servants'[8] but already by that time the cause of prison privatisation had been taken up by a group of Conservative backbench MPs and peers who lobbied for it with passionate commitment and, in some cases, became involved in the expanding security industry that resulted.[9] In 1988 the government produced a Green Paper[10] canvassing the possibility of contracting out court and escort duties and involving the private sector in the management of remand prisons. Through tortuous machinations involving a junior Home Office minister and Conservative backbench MPs the government's policy was cumulatively stretched as the Criminal Justice Act 1991 was going through Parliament, so that the Act provided for contracting out court and escort services and the management of any kind of existing or future prison. Initially the government undertook that there would be an experiment with one remand centre and that any further contracting out would await an evaluation of it. In the event that assurance counted for nothing, and in 1991 Kenneth Baker went ahead with contracting out the management of a further prison without waiting for the first one to receive any prisoners, let alone be evaluated. By early 1998, all court and escort services had been contracted out, six prisons were operated by private-sector management and staff, and in the pipeline there were five further prisons that were planned to be designed, built, financed and managed by the private sector. The private security industry has become established in the prison system in a way that was not even on the horizon 10 years ago.

Because of their financing regime and speed of construction, private prisons are very relevant to the rate at which the prison system can be expanded. It must also be inherently quite probable — though hard to demonstrate — that a powerful and profitable prison industry is likely to look

---

[8] Hansard HC, 16 July 1987, col. 1299.

[9] See Cavadino, M. and Dignan, J. *The Penal System: an Introduction*, 2nd ed. (London: Sage, 1997).

[10] Home Office, *Private Sector Involvement in the Remand System* (Cm 434) (London: HMSO, 1988).

for ways of increasing the area of its profit-making activity. There are strong views about private prisons on both sides of the argument, but we simply accept them as part of the world as it is. The Home Secretary's overall responsibility for the system is maintained through his appointment of a 'controller' in each private prison, and the reports by the Chief Inspector of Prisons make it abundantly clear that the private prisons can do an exceptionally good job. The very existence of private prisons must condition industrial relations throughout the system in a way that is unlikely to be against the public interest, and there are some ways in which the Home Office's role in them can be argued to be cleaner and more effective than it is in the traditional public-service provision. At the very least it seems clear that there are management lessons to be learned from the private prisons, and we return to this in chapter 4.

While the prison service in 1993 was getting on creditably with the job of meeting its performance targets ('key performance indicators') under agency status, the government was preparing to present itself in the spirit of a 'law and order counter-reformation'.[11] Michael Howard's 'Prison works' speech to the Conservative Party conference in October 1993 was clearly the point where the previous unspoken political consensus on avoiding an imprisonment auction was deliberately destroyed. The 'Prison works' speech not only marked the start of the present developing crisis of prisoner numbers, but also a definite change of direction towards a more austere view of prisoners' entitlements. This was given added momentum by the circumstances of the security crisis a year later.

In September 1994 a group of six category A prisoners, five of them IRA terrorists, escaped from the special security unit in Whitemoor dispersal prison, which was supposedly the most secure place in the whole prison system. The prisoners, who were all recaptured, were armed with pistols, and one prison officer was shot and wounded. When the prisoners' belongings were searched they were found to include Semtex explosive, fuses and detonators. The report by Sir John Woodcock published in December 1994[12] constituted a withering criticism of lax security, vague management and diffuse responsibilities throughout the system, and it made the prison service look ridiculous. It confirmed, for example, that the (highly dangerous and intimidatory) prisoners in the unit had established such dominance that prison officers had routinely been sent on shopping trips to buy luxury food for them. The Woodcock report noted that the special security unit had been set up when there were mixed ideologies in the prison service, which wanted to

---

[11] So called by Cavadino and Dignan in *The Penal System: an Introduction* (see note 9).

[12] Woodcock, Sir John, *Report of the Enquiry into the Escape of Six Prisoners from the Special Security Unit at Whitemoor Prison*, Cambridgeshire, on Friday 9th September 1994 (Cm 2741) (London: HMSO, 1994).

improve physical security while providing the positive inmate relationships encouraged by Woolf, and it made sweeping recommendations for tightening up security, which Howard immediately accepted. Almost unbelievably, within a month there was yet another escape from a dispersal prison, when three life-sentence prisoners escaped from Parkhurst Prison on 3 January 1995. Once again the prisoners were recaptured, but the damage to the prison service's credibility was catastrophic. A further inquiry was set up under Sir John Learmont to report on the Parkhurst escape and to review general prison security in the light of the Woodcock report.

The Woodcock recommendations had been specifically directed only to the special security unit at Whitemoor, and it had been left to the government to decide how far they should be applied to other prisons. Some of them were only applicable to dispersal prisons, but others could be of general application. In the event, there was a massive reorientation towards security throughout the prison system.

The Conservative Party conference in October 1995 was the next staging post on the road of increasingly punitive rhetoric from ministers, with Michael Howard announcing proposals for mandatory sentences for various kinds of repeat offenders. The Learmont report into the Parkhurst escape,[13] published four days after Howard's speech, made the by now customary finding of management confusion at every level, and sought to roll back penal thinking by proposing custody as the dominant aim, in replacement of Woolf's view of a balance between security, control and justice. It also proposed a total reorganisation of prison security, with a new super-maximum security prison for the highest security risks, and a new specialist control prison to boot. Howard responded by ordering a study of *two* very high security prisons and sacking Derek Lewis. The Opposition staged a debate in the House of Commons to criticise Howard's handling of the matter, but failed to make their charges stick. Lewis did rather better than that, as he sued Howard for wrongful dismissal and won an out-of-court settlement.

By this time the prison population had already exceeded its previous record level of 51,000, and the rate of increase was growing. The government cut prison running costs by 13.3 per cent over three years, but had to restore some funding in 1996 in the face of the continuing surge in numbers. By the time of the general election in May 1997, the numbers were at a new record of around 60,000 and the prison service was reduced to buying a prison ship from the USA. The House of Commons Home Affairs Committee found that the increase in prisoner numbers 'will be a major issue for the incoming government to address. Subject to this important qualification, we can be more optimistic about the future than has been possible for some time.'

[13] Learmont, Sir John, *Review of Prison Service Security in England and Wales and the Escape from Parkhurst Prison on Tuesday 3rd January 1995* (Cm 3020) (London: HMSO, 1995).

In comparison with the early 1980s the position today is obviously better in many important ways. The changes that preceded and accompanied the transition to agency status have clearly increased management effectiveness. The wretched business of slopping out has gone and the proportion of modern buildings is much higher. The uncontrolled right of the staff to take industrial action,[14] the pay structure that encouraged manipulation to increase overtime, and the daily efflux of escorting staff from remand prisons are all things of the past. The post-Woolf changes to the disciplinary system were overdue; prisoners generally have access to telephones; and the arrangements for visits have been improved.

The one issue that appears to be relentlessly heading out of control is overcrowding. The effects of this deep structural problem are amplified by the previous government's cuts on prison expenditure, and the present government's adoption of the same spending limits. The implications of all this are discussed in the next chapter.

---

[14] In *Secretary of State for the Home Department* v *Barnes* (1994) *TheTimes*, 19 December 1994, it was established that prison officers are obliged to carry out the orders of the Home Secretary, and provisions in the Criminal Justice and Public Order Act 1994 prohibited anyone from inducing prison officers to withhold their services.

4 Prisons — Protecting the Public?

Imprisonment has been a routine punishment only since the early nineteenth century. Previously, the judges came to empty the gaols, not to fill them, and the actual punishment was by way of inflicting physical pain, transportation or death. For reasons beyond those discussed in chapter 2, imprisonment is, in fact, deeply paradoxical as a form of crime control. It certainly keeps people from attacking society for as long as they are locked up, but it is inherently likely to damage them and turn them out more prone to crime than when they went in.

These points are very familiar to anyone who takes an interest in criminal justice, but not to the wider public. In all probability most of the public sees imprisonment simply as punishment and as the means of removing an offender from the streets. The idea that prisoners should be treated with 'less eligibility' — that is, with more discomfort than the poorest members of society outside — is very widespread. Few people take much interest in what happens to prisoners between the gates closing and opening on them. In fact, what happens to prisoners is vitally important not simply as a matter of civil rights and good government but also because of its likely effect on prisoners' behaviour on release.

In this chapter we make some basic points about running prisons and describe how very damaging they are if they are not run well. We firmly believe that well-run prisons can do something useful for society, in addition to containment. But high standards of prison management are very hard to maintain. If they slip, prisons very rapidly deteriorate into unruly places that can only encourage further delinquent behaviour.

Apart from specifically focused programmes aimed at controlling offending behaviour, not much has been validated about the effects of imprisonment. It is worth remembering, however, that prison involves a number of factors that are universally reckoned to lessen the chances of maintaining a law-abiding way of life. Particularly important are the separation from family and the outside world, the increased difficulty in obtaining subsequent employment and the constant exposure to other offenders. Perhaps more significant than anything else, offenders can easily drift through a prison sentence without any sense of personal responsibility, using prison as a process to avoid facing up to the reality of their offending behaviour and what it has done to other people. It may be that it has not been proved that prisons can be 'an expensive way of making bad people worse',[1] but the nature of prisons is such that it would be astonishing if that diagnosis were wrong. We believe that the Woolf report got it right in saying that, without remedial action, the natural consequence of a sentence of imprisonment will be a deterioration in the ability of the prisoner to operate lawfully within society, and that the prison service's duty is to minimise that deterioration.[2] Several countries place a duty on their prison services to seek to minimise the negative aspects of imprisonment.

We are now in a much better position to run prisons well than we were in the 1970s and 1980s, and there is a fair consensus on how to do it. The Woolf report genuinely marked a great step forward in conceptualising what a decent prison system should be like, in a way that could command general acceptance. Its core proposition of security, control and justice all requiring to be maintained, and also to be kept in balance, may seem a very simple idea, but it caught a real truth and supported the comprehensive reform programme spelt out in the White Paper, *Custody, Care and Justice*. That programme is still the prison service's basic blueprint. The prison service's statement of purpose declares that it serves the public by keeping in custody those committed by the courts and that its duty is to look after them with humanity and help them lead law-abiding and useful lives in custody and after release. That is elaborated in the service's statement of vision, goals and values, which is an aspirational document, setting out aims and commitments on virtually all important aspects of the service's responsibilities. If a prison system could live up to these statements it would set standards for the world.

Each element of Woolf's balance of security, control and justice has clearly been recalibrated since his report. There has been a very heavy new emphasis on all aspects of security following the escapes from Whitemoor and Parkhurst. The control dimension, too, has been significantly enhanced by an incentives and earned privileges scheme, tighter control of prisoners'

---

[1] Home Office, *Crime, Justice and Protecting the Public* (Cm 965) (London: HMSO 1990).
[2] Woolf, Lord Justice and Tumim, Judge Stephen, *Prison Disturbances April 1990: Report of an Inquiry* (Cm 1456) (London: HMSO, 1991), para. 14.8.

property, mandatory drug testing and increased disciplinary powers for governors. Additionally, the prison service has recognised the importance of strategies to prevent bullying, though the extent of these is difficult to establish. On the other hand, the general idea of 'less eligibility' has been encouraged by ministerial statements about the need for austerity, and the delivery of inmate programmes is now being very severely damaged by financial restraints and overcrowding. The forthright reports by the Chief Inspector of Prisons are the indispensable guide to what these things mean on the ground.

A reorientation towards security was bound to follow the catastrophic revelation that the implementation of this part of Woolf's requirements was so defective. The performance in preventing escapes and disturbances is now extraordinarily good and the confidence of staff is felt to be much higher. The important thing should be to exploit that confidence in positive ways. The overall assessment, however, must be that while the prison service has been highly successful in delivering the first (custodial) part of its statement of purpose, it has fallen badly behind on the second.

If Lord Woolf were writing his report today he would certainly want to say more about treatment programmes for offending behaviour, of the kind described in chapter 2. In 1996 the prison service committed itself to developing these by incorporating them in its key performance indicators. The service is now at the leading edge of world practice in setting up a scheme for delivering these programmes and submitting them to international accreditation, which means that if the prison delivers the programme as specified, it will reduce reconviction rates. Currently programmes exist for sex offending, drug and alcohol abuse, and the management of violent behaviour; and others are being developed. The whole scheme will be subject to validation, but there is no reason to doubt that programmes of this kind can reduce reoffending by some significant amount.

Modern offending behaviour programmes have a broader importance for prisons in that they at last provide, in a form that can be widely adopted, a credible delivery system for doing something to help prisoners lead law-abiding lives. They therefore act as a focus for a positive approach to prisoners and for active concern with prisoners as individuals. Where prison staff are involved in delivering these programmes they become highly motivated. They are not just equipped with effective new skills but are encouraged to relate to prisoners in exactly the way that the management wants to see in a well-run prison. Furthermore, offending behaviour programmes have a ripple effect in influencing the character of the entire establishment in which they are located. It is well understood that the impact of the programmes is largely negated by an unruly or unsupportive environment, and it has become common to operate them in wings or other discrete parts of a prison, where all the prisoners and staff are involved in the programme.

New-style offending behaviour programmes do not require a reappraisal of the purposes of imprisonment, so as to see reformation as a reason for sending someone to prison. But, although they so far only affect a limited number of prisoners, they do mark a very definite step away from the nihilism of 'Nothing works'.

Prisons are made such problematic places by the extreme range of offenders that they have to control, care for, and contain against their will. They range from the hardened career criminal and the violent and dangerous psychopath to the pathetic inadequate and the mentally disordered. The majority consist of quite ordinary persons who have committed offences of all kinds, and who want to get through their time as quietly as they can. Some, however, will be desperately trying to escape; some will be permanently anti-authority; many will want to carry on the delinquent unruliness that they bring from the streets; in young offender institutions many will be desperately immature and unable to control their actions; some will be suicidal. The problem for the prison service is to organise itself and its prisons so that all these disparate needs are met and society is protected. Maintaining security, order and fairness is no mean achievement and it requires a very high standard of sustained and focused management. If the management falls short and does not impose its own value system, other systems will begin to flourish. Even in the best-run prisons predatory behaviour, bullying and trafficking are never far from the surface and order can never be entirely guaranteed.

Anyone involved in running prisons knows only too well the difference between the atmosphere of a well-run prison and a bad one. In a well-run prison the security will be completely adequate for the type of inmate population, but it will not be oppressive. It will exist as a natural background to everything that goes on, and staff will be alert at all times. Both staff and prisoners will feel safe, and the atmosphere will reflect that. Services will be run professionally. There will be a general sense of well-controlled, but not over-controlled, order and purpose, and staff and inmates will be involved together in a range of activities. Decisions will be taken consistently, fairly and with as much explanation to the prisoners as possible. Both staff and prisoners will know where the boundaries are and what standards are expected of them. If force is needed it will genuinely be used as a last resort, and then at the lowest necessary level. The staff will be well trained, confident that they can deal with any eventuality, and able to manage even the most difficult prisoner sensitively but firmly. The staff will obviously know their prisoners and will be planning individual prisoners' time in the ways that will be of most use to them on release, and they will see it as part of their job to help prisoners to maintain links with the outside world. The staff will present as good role models, and that is especially important at young offender institutions. It will be clear that there is a strong investment of management at every level, and that senior staff regularly visit all parts of the prison. New ways of running the establishment better will be encouraged. There will be clear leadership from the top, and staff will identify with management objectives and know exactly how their particular work fits into the overall scheme.

A bad prison is very much the opposite. The physical security may be adequate but insufficiently monitored, and in the worst scenario this will lead to security breaches. Staff and prisoners will not be jointly involved in active routines in a way that generates dynamic security. The staff will revert to behaving as guards, and there will be antagonism between the two groups. There will be a heightened atmosphere of tension and fear, and little but the threat of force will underpin control. There will be no-go areas that the staff are afraid to enter. There will be evident idleness, little or no purposeful activity, slack routines, dilapidation, noise and dirt. There will be only a loose perception of standards and decisions will be taken arbitrarily and inconsistently. Inquiry will reveal that there is considerable violence, bullying and extortion by prisoners, sometimes with certain prisoners given tacit licence to maintain order by their own means. Disciplinary charges, including assaults on staff, will be common. There will be little evidence of leadership. There will be a cynical feeling from staff and inmates that all of this is inevitable and that talk of improvement is idealistic nonsense. At the worst, the atmosphere is one of despair.

These sketches are, of course, exaggerations. Most prisons are somewhere between the ends of the spectrum, and it will always be far harder to approach the top end of performance in a higher security prison than it is at an open establishment. It is also fair to say that the picture is never entirely uniform, and that there often are pockets of good practice in poor establishments. Nevertheless, the general types will be familiar to anyone who has spent much time working in a prison system. Furthermore, the nature of the business is such that there will be a constant risk of rapidly drifting down the scale unless very high standards of management and monitoring are maintained. The staff in the first kind of establishment can feel that they are doing as much as they can to protect the public by requiring prisoners to participate in a fair and just institution and by preparing them for release. The second kind of prison, however, is totally destructive. It is a thoroughly bad working environment for staff and entirely negative for prisoners. We do not believe that the experience of prison can be neutral; prisoners' behaviour is bound to be affected for better or for worse, and the second kind of prison is highly likely to reinforce criminal attitudes and behaviour.

These descriptions are not just abstract speculation; the reports by the Chief Inspector of Prisons make it clear that the prison system covers a very wide range of performance indeed. In a number of recent reports, the Chief Inspector has found examples of real achievement. At Wayland (1997) 'the variety of work and training available to inmates was impressive' and there was 'a strong sense of integration of all groups of staff into a purposeful and proud working group'. At Lancaster Farms (1995) 'the statement of purpose — "our aim is to prevent the next victim" — typified the positive message to inmates and staff' and most inmates 'felt that the establishment was helping them not to reoffend'. Doncaster (1996) was 'one of the most progressive prison establishments in the country' where examples of outstanding practice included 'the management of young offenders, the prison's anti-bullying policy, the care of prisoners intent upon self-harm, and the management information systems'.

Doncaster is one of the handful of privately managed prisons, and it is already beginning to be clear that these establishments tend to score well in terms of service delivery, clear management aims and the expectations of staff performance. They also tend to be innovative and to operate in a way that gives meaning to the prison service's statement of vision, goals and values. In privately managed prisons the role of the Home Office is not to provide the service itself, but to act as the client, ensuring that the provider is delivering services of the required standard. The way forward must be to find ways of adapting that dynamic to the circumstances of the traditional, publicly provided, part of the prison system.

At the other end of the scale, many recent reports by the Chief Inspector have been extremely disturbing. In one case (Lincoln, 1997) the Chief Inspector found that demoralised staff were unable to control the high level of assaults and endemic bullying in the remand wing, where 200 prisoners were unlocked every day with little to keep them occupied. In another (Wormwood Scrubs, 1997) he diagnosed 'the absence of any sort of appropriate regime for prisoners' and 'no sense of purpose in what most staff were doing'. In another (Chelmsford, 1997) he found that over 100 young offenders were housed in the same area as adults and were treated with 'an appalling and nineteenth-century attitude'. In a young offender institution (Dover, 1997) he found that the prison service had failed to 'provide a reasonably safe living environment for young offenders' and that there was 'untold bullying and criminal corruption'. Feltham young offender institution (1997) was 'a gigantic transit camp' in which 'the obligation to provide all those under school leaving age with 15 hours of education is not being met'.

When one reads of bad prison conditions one also needs to remember the kind of person who ends up in and out of prison, often having been in local authority care and then having served an apprenticeship in a young offender institution. We know[3] that there is a very strong connection between chronic early offending and a set of social and economic disadvantages. In particular, the chronic delinquents tend to come from the poorest and largest families, to be physically neglected and in bad housing, and to suffer from parental conflict and erratic child-rearing, sometimes passive but sometimes harsh and cruel. Their parents are likely to be criminal and their siblings and friends delinquent. Like their parents, they tend to be poor achievers at school; they lack concentration and often truant. In their behaviour they are impulsive and easily bored, dishonest and sensation seeking.

By definition these are the most difficult and troublesome people in society. They can be identified at an early age and there are ways of helping them and increasing their life chances by early intervention. All that we are emphasising in this chapter is that placing people from such backgrounds in the poorer kind of institution we have described cannot conceivably do anything to resolve their delinquency and thereby protect the public. Common sense dictates that the effect must be the absolute opposite, and that they will be further damaged and confirmed in antisocial behaviour.

All this was devastatingly summed up by the Chief Inspector of Prisons in his report on young prisoners,[4] produced in November 1997. As the Chief Inspector stated:

> The vast majority of young people in custody need individual attention given to the problems which produced their criminal behaviour. If all they get is akin to being stored in a warehouse, then the chances of their reoffending, creating yet more victims, is very great indeed . . . but unless they receive individual attention and opportunities to change, their time in custody will make them worse rather than better.

The Chief Inspector went out of his way to give credit to staff who were doing their best in difficult circumstances, but was, in the main, disappointed in looking for rigorous, purposeful and humane regimes. His report contained a long catalogue of examples of unacceptable and uncaring ways in which the prison service was treating the young adults and juveniles in its care. His main conclusion was the damning one that the system was so defective in meeting the needs of juveniles under the age of 18 that the responsibility of keeping them in custody should be transferred to an entirely new organisation.

The current situation has been very largely conditioned by the combination of a rapidly increasing prison population and severe financial restrictions.

---

[3] Particularly from successive reports by Farrington and West under the Cambridge Study in Delinquent Development.
[4] *Young Prisoners: a Thematic Review by HM Chief Inspector of Prisons for England and Wales* (London: Home Office, 1997).

Clearly, an injection of money would diminish some of the problems described, but the effects of long-term overcrowding cannot be resolved by money alone. As Woolf found, it has a corrosive effect on the whole system. In any event, the dynamics of overcrowding and prison expansion are such that the money to cope with the population *always* lags behind the overcrowding.

The public's idea of overcrowding is no doubt dominated by the conditions that were at the heart of the Strangeways riot — two or three prisoners confined for most of the day in a Victorian cell. Long before conditions get to that sort of unacceptable extreme, however, overcrowding has a suffocating effect on an establishment. With excessive numbers of prisoners, staff are rushed off their feet and all the normal routines like unlocking, mealtimes and searching inevitably take longer and longer. Since the basic tasks of custody have to take precedence, everything else tends to get squeezed out. An imaginative governor and staff will always try to find ways to avoid the worst effects, but a seriously overcrowded prison eventually becomes overwhelmed by the number of transactions that have to be performed, so that little is left except security and the most basic services. The establishments that are worst affected in this way will always be the remand prisons.

At the level of national management the effects of excessive numbers may be less dramatic, but they are just as debilitating. The daily business of squeezing the last ounce of capacity out of the system comes to dominate longer-term planning, and there is a permanent atmosphere of crisis management. The mix of establishments is constantly juggled in endless compromise permutations, so an adult prison has to yield a wing that can be given over to young offenders, or a prison that is used to hold long-term prisoners is required to take on a remand function. Prisoners are rushed through the allocation units too hastily, so they are not properly assessed. There is an inevitable tendency to press prisoners down the security categories so as to use all the places in the less secure prisons, which makes management and control more problematical. In order to use places wherever they appear, prisoners are moved at short notice, often to places far from their homes. This disrupts any education or training that they are receiving and causes resentment by making family visits much more difficult.

If the prison system is running properly it should be projecting criminal justice values by operating fair and orderly institutions that provide purposeful regimes and are supportive of programmes that require as many offenders as possible to address their behaviour. This is not only right in itself but it also offers the best protection to the public. In conditions of prolonged overcrowding it becomes more and more difficult for the system to cater properly for the special needs of groups, such as young offenders and women, and for the particular requirements of individuals.

Operating anywhere near the top end of the spectrum of good practice becomes increasingly difficult, and there is a remorseless pressure that forces establishments away from the prison service's commitment to help prisoners lead law-abiding and useful lives.

We are not suggesting that the situation today is yet like that of 10 years ago, but the inherent effects of excessive numbers have not changed. It is profoundly depressing for two people who worked in prison management in the 1980s to see the situation heading back in that direction.

5   International Comparisons

Before we go any further we need to stand back a little and consider how our country fits into the wider international context. The main reason for this is because of the USA's importance in setting the agenda that this country has been pursuing in recent years, but it will also be worthwhile to note the main features of the scene in Western Europe.

One has to ask right at the outset what it is that international comparisons hope to measure, and whether it is worth trying to make them. Traditionally, the single most quoted figure for international prison comparisons has always been a jurisdiction's prison population expressed as a rate per 100,000 of the general population. All developed countries have a population census system that at least provides a recognised figure for the general population, and one would think that the figure for the prison population was just as firm. In practice, matters are not quite so simple and there are problems in standardising data, mainly because of the differences in the ways that countries allocate various categories of offenders to types of institutions. Juveniles, mentally disordered offenders and immigration detainees, for example, may be held outside the prison system, or only partly within it. For the simple purposes of this book, however, that kind of problem can be regarded as marginal, and we can simply note that the traditional rate per 100,000 does have the enormous advantage of recording reasonably solid and consistent information.

The rate per 100,000 figure is, however, very limited in what it tells us. One issue that it does not touch upon is the split between prisoners being held on remand and the sentenced population, in which there are enormous differences even between Western European countries. But, above all, the traditional figure does not tell one anything at all about a jurisdiction's punitiveness. A prison population may be weighted towards long terms or short ones, and those sentences may be associated with the crimes committed in ways in which the crude rate per 100,000 figure cannot tell one anything.[1] In order to understand what the prison population really represents in terms of punitiveness it would as a minimum be necessary to obtain information about a jurisdiction's number of convictions. A proper understanding of the use of imprisonment would require knowledge of the numbers arrested, diverted, prosecuted, convicted and given non-custodial disposals. Such an analysis would clearly be a major task for each jurisdiction, and the further back the information is within a jurisdiction's criminal justice system, the greater the problem of quality control.

An alternative approach — though one that gives insight rather than proof — is to assemble an international sample of sentencers and find out what sentences they see as appropriate for illustrative offences of various kinds. Several exercises of this kind have, indeed, been mounted by the National Association for the Care and Resettlement of Offenders (NACRO) and others. They strongly tend to show that sentencing in England and Wales is generally heavier than in Western Europe.

Because of increasing awareness in recent years of the limitations of the traditional rate per 100,000 figure, the Criminal Statistics for England and Wales have adopted the practice of showing international comparisons of imprisonment rates both in the traditional way and also expressed as a ratio of recorded crime. This has the effect of showing England and Wales far lower in the Western European league table than does the traditional figure, because crime recorded by the police in England and Wales is high in comparison with most other European countries. The difficulty with this ratio, however, is that the recording of crime depends on many factors and is notoriously problematic in any jurisdiction. For example, the high English rate of recorded crimes in the European league table may have something to do with the high level of public confidence that the English police appear to enjoy, judged by European norms. A ratio between the prison population and the recorded crime rate is therefore inherently subject to the weakness that it combines a hard figure with a soft one. For that reason alone the ratio with recorded crime will not replace the traditional population ratio as the single thumbnail measure of cross-national imprisonment comparisons.

For the limited purposes of this book we will use the traditional rate per 100,000 figure from time to time, but with full appreciation of its shortcomings. The truth is that no single measure can tell one very much. The most it can do is to chart changes over time and draw attention to disparities that

---

[1]See, in particular, Pease, K., 'Cross-national imprisonment rates', in King, R. and Maguire, M. (eds), *Prisons in Context* (Oxford: Clarendon Press, 1994).

are worth investigating further. It is the investigation of the reasons for the disparities that tells us things that are worth knowing. Having said all that, the traditional per 100,000 figure does at a glance tell one the amount of incarceration that a country of a given size feels that it needs by way of punishment and to preserve its citizens' safety, and that itself is not a worthless thing to know.

In 1996 England and Wales had a figure per 100,000 population of 110, which was the same as Spain and Scotland, and appreciably higher than France, Germany or Italy, all of which had 90. In Western Europe only Portugal had a higher figure (140). The Czech Republic, Poland and Hungary had 200, 150 and 130 respectively, though the last two had fallen by more than 40 per cent in the previous 10 years. All these figures are dwarfed by Russia (710) and the USA (610).[2]

WESTERN EUROPE

It is worth making a few comments on Western Europe. First of all, the cultural and historical background to penal issues varies enormously from country to country. Second, contacts between Western European governments are not especially close on penal affairs, and there is not even a very highly developed information flow for the basic facts on prison populations. This is a direct reflection of the status (or, rather, non-status) of penal affairs in the European Union. The Union's common interest in criminal matters is confined to aspects that involve judicial and police cooperation, or which involve a specific common interest such as the prevention of fraud against the Union budget. Certainly, no common interest has been recognised, or is likely to be recognised, in prisons as such or in sentencing policy generally.

As regards those matters that are taken ahead under the auspices of the European Union, not only are there formal arrangements for gathering information but the senior officials in the ministries of justice and home affairs of the member States are meeting regularly and build up quite a deep understanding of the position in the other countries. In the case of prison matters, on the other hand, the relevant multilateral body is the Council of Europe, which now has a membership extending far beyond Western Europe, and which is manifestly a far looser kind of institution than the European Union. Some of the Council of Europe's work, especially the European Convention on Human Rights, is clearly of great relevance to prisons, but one has to say that even the flow of standardised prison information from the Council of Europe is of limited use because it is based on an annual census, which is always a year out of date.

---

[2] These are all pre-publication figures from the 1996 *Criminal Statistics*.

The upshot of all this is that English prison policy-makers have always been less interested in Europe than in the USA, to which we are so close by virtue of language and the shared common law tradition. Nevertheless, our rate of imprisonment in comparison with that of Western Europe does at least pose the question why there should be such a difference.

A few years ago, a commentator would have added that the Netherlands had a rate of imprisonment around one third of ours, and that Germany had reduced the rate of imprisonment and was actually closing prisons, but neither of those statements can be made today. Over the last 10 years the Netherlands prison population has rapidly increased to the European average of 80 per 100,000. The position in Germany is complicated by the absorption of the East German prison system, which had a very high incarceration rate. How closely rising imprisonment rates in Europe are linked with greater freedom of movement is a matter of speculation. The striking rise of imprisonment in the Netherlands, however, does seem to have been recognised there as at least partly a consequence of the policy of open borders, and partly a consequence of the pressures of international crime.

All that a comparison with Western Europe shows, then, is that England and Wales are maintaining their place near the head of the league table of imprisonment rates. We are, moreover, rapidly increasing our rate, so that the November 1997 prison population (63,500) represents a rate of more than 120 per 100,000. In April 1997 the Home Office issued prison population forecasts that showed a mid-range figure of 74,500 by the year 2005. That would represent a rate of something like 144 per 100,000, which would be extraordinarily high for Western Europe in modern times, and would put us quite high in the league table of the former Soviet bloc countries of Eastern Europe. During 1997 the actual population has in fact grown much more quickly than was forecast in April, so that we are currently on course to reach the 144 per 100,000 figure in the very early years of the new millennium.

THE USA

It is difficult to find a single convincing explanation for the vast rise in imprisonment in the USA since the prison population began to climb steeply in 1973. Clearly, the USA has long had a massive problem of homicide (which is about 15 times more frequent than in the UK) and other crimes of extreme violence, aggravated but not simply caused by inadequate gun control laws and the very widespread availability of firearms. Organised crime, too, is of a different order from that which has hitherto existed in Europe. However, the index rate for crimes of grave violence in the USA more than tripled in the 15 years before 1973, and during that period the prison population rate per 100,000 population actually declined, to reach a post-war low point in 1972.[3] The emergence of a 'get tough' attitude to law and order is, intuitively, closely linked to the course of events, but we are not aware that it has ever been demonstrated why public and political attitudes of that kind should have been different in the early 1970s from any time in the previous several years. The prison population of any country is the product both of crime and of a highly complex mix of attitudes and decisions in police forces, prosecuting authorities, courts and legislatures. While the general course of the USA's national imprisonment project is plain enough, the present short summary will not be able to bring out the differences that exist between the 50 states of the union, which in fact do pursue a wide range of crime policies and show a greater spread of imprisonment rates than exists within the European Union. It is important to remember that the bulk of US prisoners are in State prisons, which hold convicted felons serving more than one year. The federal prisons, for offenders against federal law, only hold about 10 per cent of the total. Convicted prisoners serving less than one year and people held in custody awaiting trial are held in locally run jails rather than prisons, and these are the responsibility of county or municipal authorities.

For at least the 30 years prior to 1970 the 'treatment model' had dominated US sentencing laws and structures, both at federal and state level. Apart from life for murder in some states, there were few mandatory minimum sentences (the last remaining ones in federal law being abolished in 1970). A judge would sentence a convicted offender to probation or to imprisonment for a maximum term, within the maximum for the offence that the legislature had prescribed. The release decision would then be taken by the relevant parole board, normally at some point after the prisoner had served one third of the sentence, and the prison authorities were also normally able to grant 'good time' for good behaviour, which could also be for up to one third of the maximum.

For 25 years from 1967 this country, too, had discretionary parole after one third of the sentence, with a standard rate of remission ('good time') also set at one third. The indeterminacy of the US practice was, however, far deeper and more pervasive than was ever the case here. Our judges have always been supposed to forget parole, and to give the sentence that is appropriate for the offence, whilst judges in the USA gave sentences expressed as maxima, acknowledging the paramount role of the parole boards. Just as importantly, the USA jurisdictions never developed any oversight of sentence lengths through an appeals system, since sentences were regarded as something that sentencers and parole officials magically

---

[3] Zimring, F. and Hawkins, G., *The Scale of Imprisonment* (Chicago: Chicago University Press, 1991).

discerned to be appropriate to the unique human being in front of them. As Michael Tonry has pointed out,[4] an appeal system would have been otiose as there were no rules against which appeals could have been founded or judged.

When the reaction came against indeterminacy it rapidly took off and gathered momentum, with the pressures for change coming from several directions. First, civil rights activists increasingly focused on the evident inconsistencies and disparities in sentencing and parole practice, and the racial and gender bias that went with it. The landmark publication that is always quoted in that context is *Struggle for Justice* by the American Friends Service Committee (1971), which called for controls on the extreme discrepancies in sentencing and parole practice. Aligned with that train of thought, but coming at the issue from a different starting point, legal proceduralists of the period were arguing for greater fairness and accountability in many areas of the legal system, sentencing included. In 1971 the National Crime Commission published a report criticising the indefensible vagaries of parole decisions and calling for a uniform system of federal sentencing, but the keynote text is *Criminal Sentences: Law without Order* (1972) by Judge Marvin Frankel (himself a federal district judge), who took the critique further and made recommendations for a machinery to address the problem. Specifically, Frankel argued for the establishment of a new kind of agency, a sentencing commission, that would have the duty of producing rules for sentencing. Those rules would be presumptively applicable in the courts, and their implementation would be subject to review by the higher courts.

Frankel's proposal of a sentencing commission proved extremely successful in that, by 1996, arrangements of that kind had been adopted by 25 states and the federal system. However, the nature of the rules promulgated by these commissions has varied a good deal both as regards prescriptiveness and severity, and it is important to realise that Frankel's device is no more than a value-neutral machinery or 'delivery system' to produce the end product of consistent sentencing. What sentencing norms are put into the machinery is quite another matter, and to consider that aspect we have to switch our attention to a different kind of critique of the 'treatment model' that had been building up over the previous few years, and which simply asked the question whether it 'worked' in its purpose of altering prisoners' subsequent behaviour, so as to reduce their reoffending.

The starring role of the small boy who calmly observed that the treatment model emperor happened to have no clothes is conventionally given to Robert Martinson, who wrote a famous article on the subject in 1974.[5] Given

---

[4] In *Sentencing Matters* (New York: Oxford University Press, 1996).
[5] Martinson, R., 'What works? Questions and answers about political reforms', *The Public Interest*, 10, pp. 22–54 (1974).

the conclusiveness of the finding that prison sentences of themselves had no advantage over other disposals in reducing reoffending, it is a good question why the observation had not been forthcoming before. Part of the explanation doubtless lies in the more powerful research tools that were becoming available at the time. Be that as it may, the puncturing by Martinson and others of the prison-as-treatment model had complete and overwhelming success, so that the slogan 'Nothing works' came to be widely accepted for many years, obscuring the fact that, as we saw in chapter 2, some treatments can assist some people to avoid re-offending. (In fact, Martinson himself was not the originator of the phrase 'nothing works' and he came to resile from the thought it embodies.)

Once the legitimacy of the treatment model and the indeterminate sentencing that articulated it had simultaneously collapsed, a wholesale movement got under way towards abolishing or reducing the scope of parole (in which the way was led by Maine in 1975) and the enactment of determinate sentencing laws. The first of these was the Californian Determinate Sentence Law of 1976, which specifically rejected rehabilitation as an aim of imprisonment, and stated its main goal as the elimination of disparity and the provision of uniformity. By the standards of later legislation, the California law left judges with appreciable discretion, since it did not dictate the criteria for choosing between probation and imprisonment but simply provided three levels of sentence length from which the judge should normally choose, with a presumption that the middle level should be chosen unless there were circumstances that indicated either the more severe or more lenient level. In the light of later developments it is noteworthy that the 1976 California law was welcomed at the time across the whole spread of expert and political opinion. Although civil rights activists had been provoked by the inconsistencies and unchecked racial bias of the indeterminate system, conservatives distrusted the parole arrangements as being too lenient and too much concerned with the offender's interests rather than with punishment and the protection of the public.

In the same year (1976) that saw the California determinate sentencing legislation, Andrew von Hirsch produced an influential book *Doing Justice*, on behalf of the Committee on the Study of Incarceration, which was important because it developed the analysis in *Struggle for Justice* and attempted to establish criteria for retributive punishment in the post-rehabilitation world. Thus, sentencing practice should frankly acknowledge that its purpose is to distribute punishment in accordance with the seriousness of the offence that has been committed, and the criterion should not be either the nature of the offender or a prediction of his future behaviour. From then on a burgeoning science of 'desert theory' established that the concept of proportionality in sentencing involved 'cardinal' proportionality between sentences and offences and also 'ordinal' proportionality between sentences for different offences, and it suggested theoretical approaches to issues such as the account to be taken of previous convictions and multiple convictions on the same occasion. This has always been an essentially theoretical exercise, and on several issues such as the importance of previous convictions there has continued to be dispute over the years. The ground has also changed on some of the fundamental tenets of the theory. At the time of *Doing Justice*, for example, von Hirsch believed that the material deprivations of punishment were to be justified by a theory of benefits and burdens, rather like the eighteenth-century idea of a social contract, whereby the offender paid through punishment for the wrongful advantage gained over law-abiding citizens. He later came to see that this position depended on an unrealistically rosy view of the justice of the underlying social arrangements, and he came to adopt a more straightforward approach in which the general justification for punishment lay at least partly in the prevention of crime.

The characteristic piece of technical apparatus that was developed in the flight from indeterminacy was the 'sentencing grid'. This was originally developed for the US Parole Commission for use in parole release guidelines but it has been widely adopted in structured sentencing schemes. The grid shows on one axis the seriousness of the current offence according to prescribed measurements and, on the other axis, the offender's criminal history (including, in some cases, an assessment of the risk of future recidivism). The area of the chart can then be filled in with a dividing line between custody and probation, and with sentence lengths of graduated severity, and the intersection of the readings on the two axes shows the appropriate sentence. Naturally, the pitch and placement of the dividing line reflects the importance that the compilers of the grid wish to give to the current offence as against previous convictions, and the severity of the indicated sentences is entirely a matter of choice, provided they reflect an internally coherent relationship. Also, the status of the grid's indication of sentence is itself a matter of choice. It may be mandatory on sentencers, depriving them of all discretion; or at the other end of the spectrum it may be intended as no more than a presumption that the sentencer should bear in mind.

Desert theory, and technical devices such as sentencing grids, are simply designed to improve consistency. The level of severity is a separate matter. The theorists who led the reaction from unregulated indeterminacy were predominantly believers in restraining the use of imprisonment. *Doing Justice*, for example, recommended a moderate sentencing regime, well below contemporary US norms, and made a point of suggesting that imprisonment should be reserved for the more serious felonies. From the late 1970s on, however, the one constant in the USA's ferment of activity in replacing sentencing laws was that politicians in legislatures were involved in establishing new sentencing criteria in a way that had not been generally true of the long years of indeterminate practice. One thought in Frankel's mind when he proposed the sentencing commission model was that a body of that kind would stand apart from immediate political pressure, and it was always open to a legislature to proceed in that way, by establishing a commission and not laying too heavy a controlling hand on the commission's outcome. In general, the states that have adopted sentencing commissions are probably reckoned to have managed the events of recent years with less turbulence, and less extreme politically-dictated sentencing provisions, than those that have not. However, the existence of a commission does not of itself guarantee either the aim of a moderate sentencing regime or even insulation from political pressures. The US Sentencing Guidelines Commission, established under the Sentencing Reform Act of 1984, for example, includes deterrence in its guiding principles and it produced a harsh and complex structure of sentencing guidelines that were mandatory on judges and left them to decide sentences within a very narrow range. To make matters worse, Congress has included mandatory minimum sentences in more than 60 statutes, and these have been accommodated in the guidelines by general increases across the board, rather than by simply stipulating that where there is conflict between the guidelines and a mandatory sentence the latter should prevail. Very many of the states' penal codes are now harsh and inflexible, with every state now having adopted some mandatory minimum sentences, most commonly for drugs offences.

The ways in which this escalating punitivism has specially manifested itself in the 1990s are through 'truth in sentencing' and 'three strikes and you're out'.

'Truth in sentencing' requires that a prisoner should serve a high proportion — usually 85 per cent — of the full term of his sentence. This has received some backing from judges, who felt that parole and good time were undermining sentencing decisions, but the immediate motivation for it has usually stemmed from highly publicised cases in which prisoners released early under parole or good time have committed lurid crimes. A notorious example of the political exploitation of that kind of event was George Bush's torpedoing of Michael Dukakis's presidential campaign in 1988 by publicising the case of Willie Horton, who committed a rape when on home leave from a Massachusetts prison while Dukakis was governor of the state. The 1994 Violent Crime Control and Law Enforcement Act makes federal funding available to assist prison construction programmes in states that adopt the 85 per cent restriction for violent offenders. The problem with all 'truth in sentencing' schemes is, of course, that bringing the time to be served closer to the pronounced sentence means increasing the time spent in prison unless the pronounced sentence is reduced, which is likely to be very difficult to achieve if public concern about crime is running high.

'Three strikes and you're out' is a severe type of habitual offenders penalty, requiring life imprisonment on the third conviction. The scheme — or, at least, the idea of using the baseball slogan in the context of criminal justice — was originally proposed by a radio DJ in Washington state and after the National Rifle Association had stepped in to provide campaign finance the law was enacted there in 1993 on a margin of three to one in an initiative to the people (a procedure whereby citizens can propose legislation and vote on it in a referendum). The Washington state law applies to three convictions for serious violent or sexual offences, but Congress and the numerous other states that have adopted the 'three strikes' scheme have used various criteria for the qualifying offences. The federal scheme, embodied in the 1994 Act, works by reference to a restricted range of violent or serious sexual offences and is generally reckoned to have been drawn up so as to enable President Clinton to take credit for imposing a 'three strikes' regime on federal sentencing, as he had promised in his State of the Union address, without incurring significant inflation of the federal prison population. At the other end of the spectrum, California adopted, in 1994, an extravagant version of the idea, in which the two qualifying convictions had to be for serious felonies but the final one, which actuates a sentence of 25 years to life, could be for any felony, including such common offences as car theft or the possession of drugs. The event that precipitated the California legislation was the abduction and murder of a young girl, Polly Klaas, by a prisoner who had been released after serving half of a 16-year sentence for an earlier kidnapping. The legislation therefore restricted good time to 20 per cent, combining 'truth in sentencing' with 'three strikes and you're out'. Once again, the measure was endorsed by a three-to-one popular vote and had been championed by the National Rifle Association as part of its strategy to distract attention from the mounting pressure for more effective gun control laws. Campaign finance was also provided by the California Correctional Peace Officers' Association, who looked forward to the eventual creation of 18,000 prison officer jobs flowing from the legislation. On this occasion the endorsement by popular vote came after the state's governor had already signed the legislation into law, having campaigned for it as a memorial to Polly Klaas, whose own family actually criticised the proposals because they bore so heavily on non-violent offenders.

It is hard to disentangle exactly how much of the growth of prison numbers in the USA is directly attributable to the two decades of hectic legislative activity on sentencing, predominantly in the direction of markedly greater punishment. For example, it has been demonstrated[6] that the sharp increase

---

[6] Zimring, F. and Hawkins, G., 'The growth of imprisonment in California', in *Prisons in Context* (see note 1).

of imprisonment in California in the 1980s took place mainly because of a change in sentencing practice by the courts, rather than as the direct result of the 1976 determinate sentencing measure or any other legislative cause. It is also true that several studies have shown considerable avoidance of mandatory minimum sentences by the agencies of the criminal justice system (together with their exploitation as bargaining counters by prosecutors) at the same time as widespread examples of mandatory minima leading to manifestly excessive punishment, such as the notorious case of a man sentenced to life imprisonment for stealing a pizza. For the broad purpose of this book there is no need to attempt an apportionment between the narrow effects of the various new laws and the generally punitive sentencing environment. The basic fact is that the prison and jail population of the USA has more than quintupled in the 25 years from 1970, and tripled from 1980, to stand at 1.6 million in 1996, representing a rate of 610 per 100,000 population.[7]

Not all states have participated in this surge of incarceration, but most have done so and some of the increases are remarkable. The California prison and jail population expanded fourfold during the 1980s, and continued at that rate so that the prison and jail population in 1995 was more than six times that of 1980. Texas and Colorado tripled their prison populations in the 10 years from 1986. The increase of 45,000 in Texas in the five years from 1989 was not far short of the entire prison population of England and Wales or of France.

It is often said that the emerging desert theory of punishment was hijacked by conservative proponents of 'law and order' policies, but that implies a more conscious process than probably took place. The collapse of the rehabilitation model and the development of desert theory may well have bestowed on retribution a mantle of respectability that it had previously lacked but, as we have seen, the original proponents of desert theory believed in restraint in the use of imprisonment. What seems to have happened is that it was structured sentencing mechanics rather than desert theory that presented politicians with frequent opportunities to increase sentencing levels and which oversimplified the political debate. Devices such as sentencing grids gave the impression of boiling down imponderable concerns about the best treatment of individuals to a few impersonal mathematical formulae that almost begged for the legislator's carefree upward adjustment. To that extent, the stripping away of the pretence and unfairness of the old offender-based sentencing schemes did prepare the way for the unfairness and harshness of the offence-based sentencing structures that were put in place by the law and order rhetoric that became common political coin in the 1980s.

Although there now seems to be little officially sponsored research in the USA on the effectiveness of the current scale of imprisonment,[8] earlier

---

[7] Sentencing Project, Washington DC.
[8] Zimring, F. and Hawkins, G., *Incapacitation* (New York: Oxford University Press, 1995).

phases of the project were subjected to a good deal of evaluative and theoretical scrutiny. In particular, there was an important series of federally funded studies by panels of the National Academy of Sciences, which addressed the successive emerging propositions that sought to justify imprisonment as a crime control tool after the collapse of rehabilitation theory (which was confirmed by the report of the Academy's Panel on Rehabilitation in 1979). Once again, the following summary is highly compressed, but we think it gives a fair picture of mainstream research findings.

Initially, some writers in the mid 1970s made great theoretical claims for the effects of collective incapacitation, Reuel and Shlomo Shinnar, for example, asserting that serious offences would be reduced by one third if all serious offenders were imprisoned for three years.[9] The National Academy's Panel on Research on Deterrent and Incapacitative Effects, reporting in 1978, concluded that the evidence did not warrant an affirmative conclusion regarding deterrence, and rebutted the effectiveness of general incapacitation, but noted that selectively imprisoning the worst offenders had the potential for increasing incapacitative effects and called for more research on criminal careers. The idea of selective incapacitation was pushed to national prominence largely because of the work of Peter Greenwood of the RAND Corporation, who claimed that it was possible to identify high-rate offenders through a set of distinguishing characteristics (e.g., early use of drugs) compiled on the basis of interviews with offenders in prison. Greenwood claimed that concentrating the use of imprisonment on such individuals could, for example, reduce the amount of robbery by 15 per cent while simultaneously enabling the imprisonment of 5 per cent fewer robbers. One inherent problem with any thoughts of implementing Greenwood's suggestion in practice was that some of the criteria that he proposed were based on information derived from interviews rather than public record, and would thus be a dubious foundation for prolonged incarceration. At a more fundamental theoretical level, however, the Academy's Panel on Careers and Career Criminals (1986) showed that Greenwood's proposition was fallacious in being based on imprisoned offenders, who were not necessarily representative of offenders as a whole. They drew attention to the need to take account of such factors as the replacement of an imprisoned offender by another individual and the fact that much crime was committed by groups that would not necessarily be much affected by the removal of one member. The Panel also commissioned a reanalysis of Greenwood's data, which concluded that the incapacitatory effects had been overstated, and Greenwood subsequently acknowledged that conclusion.

What happened, in effect, was that a succession of theories were put forward to justify the use of imprisonment in the post-rehabilitation world,

---

[9] Shinnar, S. and Shinnar, R., *The Effects of the Criminal Justice System on the Control of Crime; a Quantitive Approach* (1975).

and a succession of major research undertakings refuted them. It was as though the USA was carrying out an immense laboratory exercise to move through the theoretical agenda that we have set out in chapter 2. In the meantime the use of imprisonment continued its unprecedented expansion, its proponents increasingly tending to rest on the bald proposition that imprisonment must by definition put offenders out of action and throwing in greater claims for deterrent effects than could be supported by the evidence. In the absence of any alternative principled arguments, and with 'just deserts' being a two-edged sword that could be used as effectively by conservatives as liberals, incapacitation has become the dominant idea behind imprisonment in the USA.

The USA manifestly has an exceptionally high rate of homicide and very serious violence, but the rate of other offending is not remarkable. New York, for example, has a homicide rate about 10 times greater than that of London, but a burglary rate that is substantially lower than London's. It would therefore not be surprising if the scale of imprisonment in the USA was largely due to prisoner populations that were heavily skewed towards offences of extreme violence, but this is not what has happened. In fact, the proportion of violent offenders among prisoners newly committed to state prisons declined from over 40 per cent in 1977 to 29 per cent in 1993. This was caused by a general shift towards greater imprisonment for non-violent crime of all kinds, though the greatest single factor has been the vivid rise in imprisonment for drug offences.

Both of these national tendencies are very clearly demonstrated in the spectacular quadrupling of the California prison and jail population, from about 25,000 to about 100,000, during the 1980s.[10] The increases in imprisonment rates here were much greater for the less serious offences such as car theft and larceny than they were for serious offences such as robbery. In fact, the number of robbers in prison in California went up by 104 per cent during the decade while the number of people imprisoned for the less serious categories of theft increased by 565 per cent. The rise in the number of drug offenders sent to prison in California was even more dramatic, increasing fifteenfold, from 1,500 to 22,600, during the decade of the 80s.

Nationwide, the proportion of drug offenders in state prisons rose from 6 per cent in 1979 to 30 per cent in 1993. A major factor in this was the war on drugs that President Reagan declared in the congressional election year of 1986, promising that the police would attack drug offending 'with more ferocity than ever before'. A particularly important episode, following the death of a basketball star from an overdose, was the initiative by the (Democrat) Speaker of the House, Tip O'Neill, for Congress to impose

---

[10] Zimring, F. and Hawkins, G., 'The growth of imprisonment in California' (see note 5).

mandatory sentences for the sale or possession of drugs. The Anti-Drug Abuse Act 1986 was rushed through Congress without any discussion of its impact on the federal sentencing guidelines and it was followed by a similar Act in 1988 which penalises the use of crack cocaine 100 times more severely by weight than that of powder cocaine, and therefore creates extreme disparity of treatment as well as the 'sentencing cliff' that is inherent in mandatory minima. Thus, possession of 4.9 grams of crack cocaine is a misdemeanour carrying a maximum of one year, possession of 5 grams of crack attracts a mandatory minimum of five years, while the user of powder cocaine can possess up to 500 grammes before falling foul of the same mandatory sentence. The significance of this is that, while crack and powder cocaine do not appear to have significant pharmacological differences, it is crack that is favoured by blacks, while whites tend to use the more costly powdered form.[11] The federal legislation has been copied in several states.

Although US government research confirms that illicit drug use by whites and minority communities is at about the same level, blacks and Hispanics now comprise nearly 90 per cent of offenders sent to prison for drug offences. Together with the distribution and disproportionate nature of the arrest figures, this strongly suggests that the drug enforcement effort has been targeted at low-level street use in the poorest and most deprived city areas. It is quite clear that drug enforcement policy is a major reason for the fact that by 1994 no less than two thirds of the inmates of state and federal prisons were black or Hispanic. About 7 per cent of adult male African-Americans are in prison on any one day, but the proportion can be twice that in some inner city areas. Removing such large numbers of, mostly young, males from the community and cycling them through the experience of prison must inevitably have a socially destructive effect on the communities concerned, especially by jeopardising the formation of stable family units.

The steep rise in the use of prison has been accompanied by a diversion of resources from other public expenditure programmes, especially social, housing, education and training programmes of a kind that provide support and opportunity to the inner city communities where crime is disproportionately prevalent. For example, the federal budget for employment and training programmes was nearly halved between 1980 and 1993 while the federal corrections budget rose by more than 500 per cent over the same period. The combined withdrawal of social programme funding and greatly increased use of prison has, it is commonly said, made the prison the leading agency of government in dealing with the poorest inner city areas. In a journalist's catchphrase, prison is becoming 'the black housing programme'.

---

[11] For a full analysis of the impact of the drug laws on racial minorities in the USA, see Tonry, M., *Malign Neglect — Race, Crime and Punishment in America* (New York: Oxford University Press, 1995).

The states have not all gone down the same path. Minnesota, for example, was one of the first two states to legislate for a sentencing commission, in 1978, and adopted terms of reference that not only recognised desert as the main criterion but also required the availability of prison accommodation to be taken into account. The arrangement is said to have worked to general satisfaction until sensational crimes in 1989 caused the legislature to double many penalties with a consequent rapid rise in the prison population. Texas, which in 1994 had a prison and jail population of 135,000 and headed the rate per 100,000 league table with a figure of 636, has decided not to adopt sentencing guidelines, and achieves its high rates of custody simply through unusually harsh sentencing and parole decisions. Some other states, such as North Carolina, have recently become alarmed at the future expenditure and overcrowding implications of their expanding prison populations, and have put work in hand to identify ways of striking a better balance, usually by the standard policy of trying to divert non-violent offenders into non-custodial penalties.

Nationwide, there does not seem to have been any very significant slackening of the rate of growth, and in many states the public appear to regard with equanimity the inevitable diversion of resources from other public expenditure. The most extreme example of this is California, where the RAND Corporation calculated that the costs of the 'three strikes' law of 1994, if fully implemented, would absorb almost all of the state's expenditure on higher education. Although the RAND Corporation's work was produced in order to inform the debate on the forthcoming popular vote, the law still obtained a popular mandate by a margin of three to one. Now, even the Republican Governor who promoted the 1994 legislation is being accused by a Democrat opponent of being 'soft on crime'.

The California legislation also illustrated another phenomenon that has accompanied the campaign for ever greater use of imprisonment. This is the use of highly questionable cost and benefit analyses designed to demonstrate that expanding the scale of imprisonment represents good value for money. In California the Governor's office produced such an analysis purporting to show that the 'three strikes' law would save great sums notwithstanding the costing by the Department of Corrections that demonstrated that the measure would cost several billion dollars for which no provision had been made. The Governor's office's analysis arrived at its conclusions largely by attaching extremely high notional costs to each homicide and making lavish assumptions of the number of homicides that would be prevented by the legislation's incapacitatory effect. A similar kind of analysis, assuming that each incarcerated offender would otherwise have been offending at a high rate and costing each victim a large monetary equivalent, had been promoted by the federal Department of Justice in 1992, towards the end of the Bush administration. While there are many areas in criminal justice administration where cost and benefit analysis is a necessary part of decision-making, it appears quite plain that these two studies are fatally flawed methodologically and conceptually.[12] The present authors are not in a position to comment on other studies that purport to justify the expansion of prisons by claiming very high saved costs, but we are aware that conservative think-tanks in the USA continue to produce work of that kind. We are bound to say that we are very sceptical about this sort of thing since it does not seem to us that the monetised costing of crime can help on the real question, which is to decide between prison and other policy choices.

Apart from making claims for the future, the proponents of imprisonment in the USA naturally also claim that the great expansion of incarceration has already been proved to be effective in controlling crime. These claims are being made increasingly at the present time, as national crime trends have been on a downward path since about 1992, just as recorded crime rates have fallen in this country. There are, however, the very strongest reasons for thinking that the massive imprisonment project that has been carried out has not been the major determinant of the level of crime.

Any discussion of crime rates anywhere has to begin with an acknowledgement of the deficiencies of the data. In the case of the USA the Uniform Crime Reports (UCR) and National Crime Victimisation Survey (NCVS) have produced divergent results. The essential point, though, is that by any measure the consistent increase in imprisonment over 25 years is simply not reflected in the trends of crime over the period. As a broad generalisation, the level of crime rose through the 60s and 70s, began falling in the early 1980s, then rose sharply in the late 80s and early 90s with an alarming increase in crime of extreme violence among juveniles, and then began falling again to reach the (historically high) level of a decade earlier, which is where it rests now. There is no correlation to be found between that sequence and the relatively constant rise in the number of criminals who were imprisoned. The same lack of correlation is found in, for example, the fourfold expansion of the California prison and jail population, from 25,00 to 100,000, in the 80s, while the state's crime rates broadly reflected the national picture. Perhaps most decisively, the events of the last 25 years have provided, as it were, separate case studies in each of the jurisdictions of the USA, and no consistent picture whatsoever emerges. Some states that have increased their prison populations above the national average have seen a decrease in crime, but some have experienced an increase, and the same differences exist for those that have imprisoned less than the average.

Just as the proponents of prison tend to claim the recently improving crime figures as a demonstration that prison works to control crime, so the

---

[12] See Currie, E., *Is America Really Winning the War on Crime and Should Britain Follow its Example?* (London: NACRO, 1996); Zimring, F. and Hawkins, G., *Incapacitation* (see note 7).

opponents of increasing imprisonment sometimes claim baldly that the facts summarised in the previous paragraph prove that it has no effect. In fact, the obvious truth is somewhere between the two. Nobody can seriously doubt that there is an incapacitation effect to be obtained from locking up criminals, but the question is whether this is sufficiently great to make it sensible to rely on imprisonment as a central crime control policy. The gearing of doubling the prison population to achieve a 4 per cent reduction in crime, described in chapter 2, was calculated in the context of England and Wales and the corresponding ratios for US jurisdictions would be somewhat different. They would, however, be in the same general ballpark, and nothing that has happened in the USA indicates otherwise. Clearly the incapacitation of 1.25 million more people than in 1973 must, if considered in isolation, have had an incapacitatory effect equivalent to several percentage points, but that has been lost in the changes in crime rates caused by social, economic and other factors. There is, for example, general agreement that the increase in violent crime in the late 80s had a lot to do with the crack cocaine epidemic, and that the improvements seen in many cities more recently have something to do with improved policing strategies (though there is less agreement about which among a number of strategies are the ones that are producing the benefits). Demographic changes and reduced unemployment are also highly relevant. In 1993 the National Academy of Sciences Panel on Understanding and Control of Violent Behavior (which reviewed both deterrent and incapacitation effects) noted that the average prison time served for violent offences had tripled between 1975 and 1989 and concluded that this increase in the prison population had apparently had very little effect on levels of violent crime. The subsequent further increase in prison numbers and reduction in violent crime does not invalidate that finding.

At this point one has to recognise the unreality of basing policy choices on the incapacitatory effects of imprisonment considered 'in isolation'. In the real world, it has only been possible to obtain whatever incapacitatory effect has been obtained in the USA at the cost of massive diversion of social programme expenditure and greatly increasing the proportion of individuals, especially from racial minority communities, who are cycled through the prison experience. It is impossible to quantify the effect that these changes have in promoting the poor social conditions that encourage crime, but it is very hard to believe that it has not been significant.

Lastly, the great increase in prisoner numbers has led to many episodes of severe overcrowding, so that very many of the states' prison systems have been subject to oversight by the federal courts at various times for breaching the constitutional prohibition of cruel or unusual punishment.

At the present time it seems that, both nationally and in the majority of states, the American people and politicians are entirely comfortable about the country's high imprisonment policy. Politicians running for office routinely try to target their opponents for being soft on crime and produce new proposals to demonstrate their own toughness, but there is virtually no questioning in political discourse of the idea of a high imprisonment policy, which is now locked into national politics by the federal grant provisions for prison construction. Law and order was originally made a campaign issue by Republican politicians such as Senator Goldwater and President Nixon, but demands for tougher penalties are now just as likely to be made by Democrats. Some states are becoming anxious about the future expenditure implications. In general, though, the prison boom seems set to continue indefinitely, notwithstanding the evident facts about the limitations of imprisonment as a way of controlling crime, mounting evidence of the unfairness of mandatory penalties, the disproportionate impact on minorities, the logjams that mandatory penalties are causing in court systems by discouraging guilty pleas, the transfer of effective sentencing discretion from judges to prosecutors, and the rising demand made by prisons on public resources.

Finally, there is the economic dimension. The number of prisoners in the USA, together with the almost equal number of people employed to guard them, is equivalent to about 4 per cent of the adult male labour force of the country. That is an extraordinarily high proportion to be diverted from wealth-producing activity, and it amounts to a real distortion of the economy and the labour market.

6 Sentencing and the Courts

The basic problem that this book revolves around is simply that, for 40 years or more, it has not been possible to align sentencing policy with the capacity of the penal system in any way that the judiciary will accept. In crude terms, the courts have usually overfilled whatever prison capacity has been available, and whenever new types of non-custodial penalties have been provided to relieve pressure on the prisons, they have been largely used to punish people who would have previously received a more lenient disposal. This dislocation — which an ex-Permanent Secretary of the Home Office described as 'a major geological fault' in evidence to the Woolf inquiry — is doubtless common to all democracies, but in the United Kingdom we experience it to an extreme degree. In part 2 we describe the main government interventions in sentencing policy since 1980, which have conditioned the present position. This chapter sets out the background. (Although the number of remand prisoners is a very important matter, we shall only make passing references to bail, which raises special questions of its own.)

The number of sentenced people in prison is linked only very remotely to the amount of crime. It is a function of the number of people convicted by the courts, the sentences passed on them, and the early release arrangements that are in force. The number of cases that come to court is controlled by the capacity of the agencies handling them, and the nature of the low-visibility choices that they make. For years past the Home Office Research and Statistics Department has drawn attention to the extent to which cases are diverted or lost at all stages of the criminal justice system, so that only 2 per cent of the offences that are committed result in a conviction. Sentencing is not the only significant gateway to punishment, though it is certainly the most visible one. In the present situation it is also the most important one; during the 1990s the number of people convicted of the more serious (indictable) offences has *fallen* by about 10 per cent but the prison population has oscillated and now surged up to record levels. Before going on to focus on sentencing and the sentencers it is worth commenting on the other main participants, and how they are related.

The Home Secretary is directly responsible for the prisons and has a general responsibility for the police and for the probation service, both of which are organised on a regional basis and are overseen by special committees established for the purpose. He is also responsible for keeping the criminal law under review and making proposals to Parliament for any changes to it. The Attorney-General is the government's legal adviser and he is responsible for the Crown Prosecution Service (CPS), which is headed by the Director of Public Prosecutions. The Lord Chancellor is responsible for the courts, for the arrangements for appointing judges and magistrates, and for civil law. Under our peculiar constitution he is also the country's head judge and the Speaker of the House of Lords. Also in the House of Lords are the Lord Chief Justice and a handful of other very senior judges (the Law Lords) who make up the House of Lords when it is sitting in its judicial capacity as our highest appeal court. They stay on as members of the House of Lords after their retirement as judges.

In the order in which an offender's case proceeds, then, the main components of the system are the police, the CPS, the process of trial and sentencing by judge or magistrates, and then the sentencing disposal to prison or to one of the non-custodial punishments that are run by the probation service. Additionally, the Department of Health is involved if there is a question of mental illness, and local authorities have special functions for juveniles. As we noted in chapter 3, one of the Woolf report's recommendations was for the establishment of a Criminal Justice Consultative Council, which has since done some useful work and which does provide a national and regional forum for the main players, though its terms of reference are limited.

The component parts of the system have strikingly different cultures, and their public visibility and expertise in managing the media is also very different. The ministers involved, together with their departments' information officers, can be expected to be highly interested in managing a news story, with the Home Secretary of the day probably being seen as more deeply versed in these arts than his specialist legal colleagues, the Attorney-General and the Lord Chancellor. The police have always had a high media presence, both through senior officers of the 43 police forces and through the office-holders of their national organisations. They are also free with the release of information in support of their campaigns, usually for heavier law enforcement. The 1991 campaign about offending on bail, for example, is a well-documented occasion when police forces released information that varied in statistical quality between the excellent and the questionable.[1] The prison service, being directly responsible to the Home Secretary, has nothing like as much autonomy for dealing with the media as the police enjoy. There have been times when the prison service has been authorised to encourage media access in order to publicise the poor conditions in prisons, but there is a clear limit to the extent to which prison service officials can go in, for example, publicly criticising a government for deliberately encouraging a high imprisonment policy that overcrowded the prisons. The belief that agency status would give the service more freedom in such matters may have been held by some people who favoured the change of status at the time, but it was manifestly illusory. The probation service is organisationally closer to the police model than to the prison one. It is a lower-profile operation than either, however, and the expression of its views in the media (usually through the channel of one or other of its staff associations) always risks appearing to be defensive of interests that are under threat. There is always a special kind of gap between the judiciary and others in the criminal justice system not only because of their constitutional position but also because of their high status as individuals and their lack of any sort of administrative infrastructure that can reliably reflect their views. Additionally, there is a notable gap in terms of culture and working experience between the judges in the courts and the officials in the Home Office who advise Home Office ministers on the criminal law. The officials do not come from a lawyers' culture, and they usually have not experienced day-to-day life in the criminal courts. All these things have had a bearing on the way in which prison and sentencing policy has been tossed to and fro over the last 20 years.

People are sent to prison either by magistrates or by the Crown Court. Broadly speaking, magistrates are responsible for most of the prisoners who are kept in custody awaiting trial, and they are also responsible for about 13 per cent of the population of sentenced prisoners.[2] The remaining 87 per cent of sentenced prisoners have been sent to prison by the Crown Court. The numbers of people sentenced to imprisonment in any year by each level of court are much more equal, but sentences are much longer in the Crown Court. In 1996 the average sentence for adult males convicted of indictable offences was three months in the magistrates' courts and 23.5 months in the

---

[1] Morgan, R. and Jones, S., 'Bail or jail?' in Stockdale, E. and Casale, S. (eds), *Criminal Justice under Stress* (London: Blackstone, 1992).
[2] Home Office, *Prison Statistics, England and Wales 1994* (Cm 3087) (London: HMSO, 1994); 'Cautions, court proceedings and sentencing, England and Wales 1996', *Home Office Statistical Bulletin* 16/97 (London: Home Office, 1997).

Crown Court. In terms of filling up the prisons one sentence of three years is the same as 18 sentences of two months.

The most serious ('indictable only') offences can only be tried in the Crown Court and the least serious ('summary') ones only by magistrates' courts. There is a large category of 'either way' offences that can be tried by magistrates if both the accused and the magistrates agree, but which otherwise go to the Crown Court. It includes many common offences like burglary that can attract heavy sentences for the most serious cases. The term 'indictable offences' covers both either way and indictable only ones, and it is usually the most convenient category to use in discussing more serious crime. The maximum sentence that a magistrates' court can pass is six months' imprisonment for one offence or a total of 12 months for consecutive sentences. The Crown Court's sentencing power is restrained only by the maximum for each offence on which the defendant is convicted.

There are about 30,000 magistrates who are part-timers without legal qualifications, though they have the services of a qualified clerk. There are also about 80 legally qualified stipendiary magistrates in London and other major cities. A magistrates' court is usually comprised of three magistrates; stipendiary magistrates sit alone. In the Crown Court, where trials are before a judge and jury, there are around 1,000 judges of various kinds. Most of them are full-time circuit judges, some are part-time recorders or assistant recorders, a few are High Court judges who try the most serious cases and have other responsibilities. Very few of the judges are women; most are white and were educated at one of the older universities.

We are profoundly fortunate in this country to have judges who are highly talented people, committed to doing justice. Nevertheless, it is worth commenting that in some countries the duties of judges and the way in which they are appointed do more to involve them with other parts of the criminal justice system than is the case here. In some, judging is a lifetime career that is entered at quite a young age and which involves extensive training. In others, a lawyer's career in the public service may involve moves between the bench and administrative appointments in the Ministry of Justice or elsewhere. It is also not uncommon for judges to have responsibilities for visiting prisons and other penal facilities in some kind of overseeing capacity. In our country judicial appointments are made comparatively late in a legal career and the training that judges receive about other parts of the system is still quite limited. Although a few judges are particularly interested in prison matters and make a point of visiting prisons, that is not a necessary part of the job.

The points in the previous paragraph are no more than an aside. What is an undoubted fact is that attitudes to sentencing in this country have developed in a way that has placed the entire subject within the independent competence of the judiciary to an altogether extreme degree. This is paradoxical, since sentencing is a completely different kind of activity from the judges' essential tasks of enunciating the law, deciding between parties to actions and supervising trials. In a free society those functions have to be exercised by a judge, but (although we do not advocate it in practice) sentencing could in theory be put in the hands of an independent body of non-judicial experts without violating any basic constitutional rule.

The reason why sentencing policy has become perceived as such an exclusively judicial preserve in the United Kingdom is very largely due to the way in which Parliament has legislated — and refrained from legislating — since the mid-nineteenth century. During that period minimum and mandatory sentences were removed for all offences except murder.[3] The result has been that sentencers have generally been restricted only by the maximum penalty prescribed for each offence, which is all that Parliament customarily now does to indicate the relative seriousness of offences.[4] This conferment of discretion has been complemented more recently by a conscious approach to the statutory definition of offences so as to define them more broadly with the intention of reducing the scope for equivocal technical argumentation in court. The Theft Act 1968 is a good example of this kind of legislation, replacing a number of old narrowly defined offences by a much smaller number of broadly defined ones in which a wide band of offending behaviour is lumped together under the same maximum penalty. In the absence of detailed Parliamentary intrusion, the judges have become more and more established as the sole custodians and guardians of everything to do with sentencing, which many felt to be a subject that had been delegated to them in its entirety. Through their exercise of an enormously wide discretion they became the effective makers of sentencing policy. There are, in fact, good reasons for entrusting sentencers with discretion so as to fit the sentence to the particular circumstances of a case. (The alternative is the rigidity of mandatory sentencing which we criticise elsewhere in this book.) That does not mean, however, that sentencers have established some right to be free from any regulation about the way in which their discretion should be used.

The judges' feeling of sole ownership of sentencing, and their methods of defending their territory, were at the heart of events in the Criminal Justice Act 1991 and the Crime (Sentences) Act 1997, which we describe in part 2.

---

[3] The mandatory driving disqualification for drunk driving, and disqualification under the totting-up procedure, were quoted in debate on the Bill which became the Crime (Sentences) Act 1997, but these withdrawals of a licence are different in kind from minimum or mandatory punishments such as imprisonment.
[4] With some short-lived exceptions such as the 1961 Criminal Justice Act's structuring of sentencing of young offenders and the 1967 Act's requirement that sentences of less than six months should be suspended unless they met certain criteria.

The debates on the 1997 Act also showed how the issue of judicial discretion had often got tangled up with totally different ideas, so that some members of Parliament opposed the government's proposals on the grounds that they breached the doctrine of separation of powers and independence of the judiciary. These ideas were sufficiently current for several senior judges to feel it necessary to go out of their way to refute them. Nevertheless, it is remarkable that the question should ever have arisen. Respect for the independence of judges in their involvement with individual cases is obviously fundamental to our democratic system, but that has nothing to do with the point. It has always been absolutely clear that there is nothing remotely unconstitutional in Parliament legislating to construct a sentencing policy by taking back some of the discretion that the judiciary have been given. There are many ways in which this might be done, such as requiring minimum sentences for specified offences, setting out the principles on which sentences should be based, or defining offences in a detailed fashion with finely calibrated sentences for each offence. The 1997 Act took the first of these routes and the 1991 Act the second. Such interventions may be wise or unwise, and the judges may respond to them (and have, in fact, done so) in ways that have been characterised as 'destructive interpretation', but there is no question about Parliament's supreme ability to make the law.

It follows from all this that there is a peculiar paradox in the relations between the executive government and the judiciary on sentencing policy. Ministers have no right to impose their wishes or even force their opinions on the judges, and they cannot go very far in public comment without risking the appearance of a damaging split, but they can always use the ultimate weapon of proposing legislation to limit the judges' discretion. And the fact is that those proposals will become law if the government has a working majority in the House of Commons and time enough at its disposal. For their part, the judges will typically see themselves as committed by their oath to do justice in the individual cases brought before them, and will be unsympathetic to the government's concerns with resources and the maintenance of viable systems.[5] Even if senior judges should agree with the government's thinking, it has never been easy to deliver a change of sentencing practice, since each judge is independent and there is every reason to believe that in sentencing it is judicial attitudes that are the key thing.

Apart from having been left in possession of the field by the abstention of the legislature, there were other reasons why the judiciary should have an exceptionally strong feeling of sole ownership of sentencing policy. Sentencing is a very demanding function, in which the decision-maker has to make the best judgment possible of a large number of factors that are of quite different kinds and which commonly pull in different directions. Lord Chief

---

[5] See Lord Justice Browne-Wilkinson's comments on economic constraints in 'The independence of the judiciary in the 1980s', *Public Law*, p. 44 (1988).

Justice Lane once said that it 'consists in trying to reconcile a number of totally irreconcilable facts'.[6] Given the history of unbridled discretion, it is not at all surprising that judges have commonly felt that sentencing was something so special and mysterious that it could be understood only by people who had heard the infinite variety of courtroom stories, and had known the unique responsibility of sentencing — in other words, themselves. That attitude, however, is not far from complete isolationism and resistance to scrutiny. The classic statement of this is the following comment by Lord Lane in 1984, when vetoing further study of Crown Court sentencing by Andrew Ashworth and associates:

> research into the attitudes, beliefs and reasoning of judges was not the way to obtain an accurate picture: sentencing was an art and not a science, and the further judges were pressed to articulate their reasons the less realistic the exercise would become.[7]

This kind of opposition to properly conducted research has had the regrettable effect that very little is known about judges' attitudes to sentencing or the way in which they approach the task in practice. As evidence about disparity in sentencing accumulates, there is an increasingly clear need for better understanding of the whole process.

Although sentencing is probably the court activity that is of most interest to the man in the street, it has historically been the poorest of poor relations of legal activity in terms of the development of reasoned principles, and it was very late to develop. Appeal in criminal cases was only established in 1907 and while the Court of Appeal[8] did settle basic procedural principles for its own use, it generally confined itself to checking that trial courts had not gone outside the wide bounds of the informal courtroom 'tariff' that was reckoned to represent what different offences merited in terms of retribution and deterrence. The scope for this was in any event severely limited because the Court of Appeal's judgments on sentencing were not reported until some selected summaries began appearing in the *Criminal Law Review* in 1954. This meant not only that there was little material available for systematic analysis, but also that sentencers in the trial courts were not even made aware of the Court of Appeal's thinking. All this was to change during the 1970s and 1980s, when several important and interlocking developments took shape.

---

[6] Hansard HL, 27 April 1987, col. 1295.
[7] Ashworth, A., Genders, E., Mansfield, G., Peay, J. and Player, E., *Sentencing in the Crown Court: Report of an Exploratory Study* (Oxford: Oxford University Centre for Criminological Research, 1984).
[8] From 1907 to 1966 the Court of Criminal Appeal, thereafter the Court of Appeal (Criminal Division).

In 1970 the first edition was published of Dr David Thomas's textbook, *Principles of Sentencing*, which was a landmark on the road to systematic examination of sentencing in this country. This was based on the analysis of reported and unreported Court of Appeal cases and, for the first time, sought to establish a comprehensive account of the sentencing practice that the court appeared to endorse. It was essentially an empirical exercise that was concerned to establish the perceived tariff for the main offences and the factors that were accepted as being especially relevant in aggravation and mitigation for them. Further important steps were the establishment of a regular systematic series of appeal reports in 1979 and the encyclopaedia, *Current Sentencing Practice* in 1982; the latter collates and classifies reported cases according to their subject.

In 1978 the Judicial Studies Board was established to provide training for judges, though use of the word 'training' was considered offensive at the time. The Board's initial focus was largely on sentencing and that interest has been retained, though it has subsequently greatly expanded its activities. Nowadays lawyers who wish to become judges exercising criminal jurisdiction will be expected to attend an induction seminar by the Board before sitting as assistant recorders for a probationary period, and if they continue as judges they will attend a refresher seminar every five years. The Board, which is chaired by a very senior judge, also provides a forum for academic lawyers and Home Office officials to discuss matters of common interest (such as future legislation) with the judiciary.

During the 1970s Lord Justice Lawton began to pioneer the use of guideline judgments in the Court of Appeal. These went beyond the immediate issues of the instant appeal in order to spell out the range of the appropriate tariff for the offence in question, and weight to be attached to the aggravating and mitigating factors that were specific to it. When Lord Lane became Lord Chief Justice he took up the technique and it has since been used on a few dozen occasions. Some of these have been intended to reflect changing social attitudes calling for greater censure of particular offences, such as rape and causing death by dangerous driving. The guideline judgment in the case of *R* v *Stewart*[9] was unusual in justifying lower punishment than had become customary (for social security fraud).

By the early 1980s, then, the Court of Appeal had at last been given memory of its own decisions on sentencing; the subject had been accepted as a proper matter for judicial training; David Thomas's work in particular had cleared away the brushwood and provided the categorisation that was needed to enable any progress towards more structure and consistency; and the court had invented the new tool of guideline judgments. It soon became clear, however, that the court's development was effectively stuck at that

---

[9] (1987) 9 Cr App R (S) 135.

point. While it continued to use guideline judgments to assist trial courts on some of the most difficult offences, such as rape and drug dealing, the focus of the court's attention was patchy, pragmatic and arbitrary. There was no attempt to construct relationships between the appropriate sentencing for offences of quite different kinds, much less to codify a core of principles that would inform all sentencing decisions. In short, the court was locked into its function as an appeal court. It was unable — in the eyes of its critics, at least — to break out of this and take on the constructive role of placing sentencing on a proper basis of coherent propositions.

There was no shortage of critics, either, since sentencing in England was rapidly becoming a subject of increasing interest to academic lawyers, who generally approached the matter on the basis of the desert theory that had been pioneered in the USA. Different scholars involved in this movement naturally had different interests, and some were more purist than others on such matters as the approach to previous convictions that was to cause so much trouble in 1993. The core proposition of the school, however, was that sentencing should be based on retribution that was proportional to the harm that an offender had done and to his culpability, and that if other considerations displaced that approach they should do so through the conscious application of consistently applied principles. From that it was possible to construct a coherent framework of criteria in which all kinds of offence would have a place, and some scholars suggested such models to take the discussion forward.

The one thing that was anathema to all proponents of desert theory was that sentencers should pick and choose from any of the rationales for punishment outlined in chapter 2 of this book. Sentences based on the four principles of retribution, deterrence, incapacitation and reform will probably be very different from each other and a desert theorist sees it as simply unjust for sentencers to pick subjectively from this menu, since it will inevitably mean that like cases are not treated alike. It also means that there are insufficiently clear criteria for the exercise of an appeal function. Such unregulated discretion leaves it to individual sentencers to make up penal policy on the wing. This 'cafeteria'[10] approach was, however, exactly what was revealed by the guide to structured sentencing that the Judicial Studies Board issued to magistrates in the 1980s. This recommended magistrates to begin their consideration of each case by deciding which aim of sentencing they wanted to follow, and nothing at the time from the Court of Appeal suggested a more rigorous approach.

The shortcomings that critics alleged about the Court of Appeal boiled down to the following. First, in the absence of a clearly stated view on the aims of punishment, there was no basis on which the court could secure consistency, much less attempt to review the proportionality of sentencing

---

[10] Andrew Ashworth's sobriquet in *Sentencing and Criminal Justice* (London: Butterworths, 1995).

between offences of different kinds. Second, although the court did offer some guidance on general issues of sentencing, this was done in an unsystematic and patchy way. There was therefore no comprehensive and coherent guidance on common sentencing issues such as the weight to be attached to a good record, the treatment of multiple convictions, the principles governing concurrent and consecutive sentencing, and the factors that should be accepted as relevant to mitigation. Third, because of the nature of its workload, the court's guideline judgments concentrated on serious offences and there was little guidance on common offences such as burglary, theft and deception. In particular, since appeals from magistrates' courts were heard in the Crown Court and did not reach the Court of Appeal, very little of the Court's pronouncements was relevant to levels of offence that were tried by magistrates. (The Magistrates' Association itself took action on this in 1989 by issuing its own national guidelines for 25 common offence categories.)

The leading figure in the criticism of English sentencing practice and the Court of Appeal's role was Andrew Ashworth. In his seminal work, *Sentencing and Penal Policy* (1983), Ashworth mounted a comprehensive attack on the existing arrangements and proposed the establishment of a sentencing council that would fill the vacuum left by the Court of Appeal's apparent limitation to a gradual, evolutionary approach. Ashworth envisaged that the council would complement the Court of Appeal and consist of judges and representatives of some other parts of the criminal justice system under the chairmanship of the Lord Chief Justice. Its remit would be to formulate and keep under review guidance for the courts on sentencing matters, including both general sentencing principles and proportionality between offences. Ashworth worked out a possible operating method for the council in some detail and went out of his way to explain the proposal impartially to the major political parties. This idea for a 'delivery system' for principled sentencing came to be adopted by all penal reform groups for several years. It was also supported by the Labour Party, who unsuccessfully tried to get it inserted into both the Criminal Justice Acts of 1988 and 1991 by amendments in the House of Lords. The judiciary's attitude was presumably accurately reflected by Lord Lane in speaking against the proposal on the first of these occasions when he said:

> It is neither a Parliamentary body nor a judicial body. . . . It is introducing a concept into the law which creates a very dangerous precedent for the future. It is removing a large portion of the independence of the judiciary and putting in its place something of which it is very difficult to see the end.[11]

---

[11] Hansard HL, 26 October 1987, col. 327.

Before moving on to the detailed account of events in part 2, there are three important issues that we want to stress.

The basic proposition that has underpinned the argument for improved structuring of sentencing is that inconsistent sentencing is unjust, but for a long time there was little evidence about sentencing disparities in the Crown Court. The situation in magistrates' courts was different, since they had a long tradition of cooperation with researchers and several studies going back to the early 1960s had revealed extremely large disparities between the sentencing norms in different court areas. From the early 1990s, however, information about Crown Court sentencing has steadily become more available, showing that the imprisonment rates of Crown Court centres of the same level can differ by a ratio of nearly two to one. It would be unrealistic to expect very close conformity in sentencing, but disparities of that order do appear, in the absence of any special explanation, to be unreasonable.

Second, as we have said more than once, consistency is only one measure of reasonable sentencing, and it is a totally separate question from severity. If all the disparities between magistrates' courts and between Crown Courts were magically ironed out so that all sentences regressed to the appropriate mean, the prison population would by definition remain exactly the same. Disparity of sentencing is a very bad thing, but it is the *weight* of sentencing that overloads prisons.

Third, there are effectively three sentencing tariffs in operation by magistrates, the Crown Court and the Court of Appeal respectively. The difference between the magistrates' courts and the Crown Court was demonstrated by a study[12] which showed that on a matched sample of cases the Crown Court was nearly three times as likely to give immediate custody and to sentence for two and a half times as long. The Court of Appeal's workload is made up of appeals against allegedly high sentences passed in the Crown Court, plus only a small number of references in cases where the Attorney-General believes that sentencing was too lenient. The Court's experience is therefore heavily biased towards the upper end of sentencing, and the previous experience of the judges in the Court is likely to be such that they have not dealt with run-of-the-mill lesser offences for a long time, if ever. It is generally believed that the Court operates the highest tariff of all and that it takes a view of less serious offences that is markedly more severe than that of the lower courts, especially the magistrates' courts.

[12] Hedderman, C. and Moxon, D., *Magistrates' Court or Crown Court? Mode of Trial Decisions and Sentencing* (Home Office Research Study No. 125) (London: HMSO, 1992).

PART 2

POLICY IN THE 1980s AND 1990s

7 Early Release and Structured Sentencing; the Criminal Justice Act 1982

Although the Conservatives had fought the 1979 election on a law and order ticket, the reality of the state of the prisons (and doubtless the character of the Home Secretary, William Whitelaw) soon steered the government into a careful posture on the use of imprisonment. The director general of the prison service was authorised to publicise the conditions caused by overcrowding, famously calling the state of local prisons 'an affront to civilised society';[1] the prison department encouraged media access to prisons for the first time, resulting in television programmes that gave a realistic picture of life inside; and Whitelaw himself made several speeches intended to 'talk down' the prison population. These were on general lines that went back at least to the time when R.A. Butler had been Home Secretary, giving reassurance that long sentences were needed for the most serious criminals but questioning the need of imprisonment and the length of sentencing for minor property offenders. He was joined in this exhortation by the newly appointed Lord Chief Justice, Lord Lane, who handed down two important judgments (*Upton* and *Begum Bibi*)[2] in the Court of Appeal, focusing on the need for shorter sentences for less serious habitual offenders. How much effect all this had is debatable. On close reading the message of the *Upton* and *Begum Bibi* judgments was not quite as liberalising as may have at first appeared, and the

---

[1] *The Work of the Prison Department* (London: Home Office, 1980).
[2] *Upton* (1980) 71 Cr App R 102; *Begum Bibi* (1980) 71 Cr App R 360.

slight reduction in sentence lengths that followed the judgments was not concentrated in the type of offence to which the judgments had been directed. Nevertheless, it broke entirely new ground for a Court of Appeal judgment (*Upton*) to recognise overcrowding in the local prisons as a factor that was relevant to sentencing because it made imprisonment 'a very unpleasant experience indeed', and for a brief moment people working in the prison system certainly did have the warm feeling that this could just be the dawn of a new era in which sentencers took account of the realities of the prisons.

The reason why the Criminal Justice Act 1982 figures prominently in this book is because it included two provisions that came to assume a lot of importance in the story of attempts to manage the overall prison population, but these were both incidental late additions to the Act's main purpose, which was to restructure sentencing and penal institutions for young offenders (i.e., 'young adults' aged from 17 to 20 inclusive, and 'juveniles' from 10 to 16). The background to this was quite complex, and is a good example of changing penological fashions. At the time of the 1979 general election young offenders could be sent to detention centres and borstals, and there was also provision for imprisonment for young adults and long-term detention for juveniles who had committed very serious offences. Detention centres were short-term (three to six months) institutions that were supposed to provide a brisk regime as a deterrent, while borstal training was a semi-indeterminate sentence between six months and two years, with the trainee released at the discretion of the institution's staff. Borstal, which was based on thorough-going reformative principles, was the nearest this country ever got to the indeterminate sentencing of the USA, though its maximum of two years was pretty mild stuff by American standards. Although borstal had been regarded as the jewel in the crown of the penal system throughout the inter-war years, by the 1980s it had become a clear victim of the movement against rehabilitation-based sentencing and the measurement of reconviction rates. Detention centres, paradoxically, were thought to have absorbed some of the aspirational elements of borstal at the expense of toughness. As early as 1974 the Advisory Council on the Penal System had recommended that the confusing menu of sentences should be replaced by a single determinate sentence of youth custody.

The background was made even more confusing by the fact that the Children and Young Persons Act 1969, which was never fully implemented, had set out an agenda to change the emphasis to welfare and to deal with many more young offenders through civil care proceedings. In the event, sentencers felt that supervision and care orders under the 1969 Act left them with no real control over what happened, and this was one reason why custodial sentencing of young offenders steadily increased through the 1970s. This trend was on top of the demographic increase in the age group, so that the number of male young offenders given custodial sentences almost doubled from about 20,000 in 1972 to about 36,000 in 1982. A further element in the situation was the fact that magistrates could not themselves pass a sentence of borstal training, but had to submit recommendations to the Crown Court, which often rejected the recommendation and imposed a lesser sentence, thereby encouraging magistrates to sentence young adults to short sentences of imprisonment when they might previously have made a recommendation for borstal (juveniles could not be sentenced to imprisonment). The combination of dissatisfaction in the courts, excessive numbers in custody and confusion of sentencing rationales had got to the end of the road, and there was general clamour for reform.

In essence, the Conservative government adopted the Advisory Council's recommendation for a single determinate sentence of youth custody, which was the first significant move in the direction of offence-based 'just deserts' sentencing reform in this country. There was, however, one high-profile exception from the Advisory Council's recommendations since the Conservative election manifesto had promised to retain detention centres and to give them a shake-up in order to deliver a 'short sharp shock' to unruly young people. Two detention centres were reorganised on that philosophy in 1980, with plenty of shouting by staff, PE and military-style drill (which the trainees actually rather enjoyed), and two more were converted later. In the event, the Home Office's evaluation of the experimental regimes showed that they were no more effective than normal detention centres in influencing reoffending and the experiment was soon dropped, though some features of the experimental regime, not including the drill, were extended to all the other detention centres.

STRUCTURED SENTENCING

One effect of the Criminal Justice Act 1982 was to increase magistrates' powers to sentence young offenders to custody, and penal interest groups were worried about this. As originally introduced, the Bill for the Act simply carried over to the new forms of custody some old provisions which restrained courts from passing sentences of imprisonment on young offenders unless they were of the opinion that no other method of dealing with them was appropriate. It was manifest that they had not had much effect, since young adults had been the fastest growing sector of the entire prison population since the provisions had been applied to them. The lead in pressing for a stronger set of requirements was taken by the Parliamentary All-Party Penal Affairs Group (PAPPAG), which had been set up under the chairmanship of Robert Kilroy-Silk MP. He introduced an amendment to the

Bill to restrict the reasons on which a court could make a decision for custody, but it was widely opposed because it did not appear to give sufficient weight to the gravity of the current offence. In the House of Lords, Lady Faithfull put forward an expanded version of the Kilroy-Silk amendment, including the idea of seriousness, and this was carried against the government. As enacted, section 1(4) of the Criminal Justice Act 1982 prohibited a court from sentencing a young offender to custody unless it was of the opinion that no other method of dealing with him was appropriate for one of three reasons. These were the offender's unwillingness or inability to respond to non-custodial penalties, the protection of the public, and the seriousness of the offence.

When Elizabeth Burney carried out research on the effect of these restrictions in magistrates' courts during the first year of the Act's operation[3] she found that although sentencers and court officials generally regarded the new rules with goodwill there was a very great deal of confusion in their minds about all three limbs of the new test, and she concluded that 'there is good cause to be pessimistic about the effects on sentencing of the provisions which are supposed to limit the justifications for custody'. Even in 1983, however, the number of juveniles given custodial sentences had begun to fall, and this trend accelerated sharply through the 1980s. A similar, though less pronounced, fall happened rather more slowly with young adults. Taking the two groups together, the virtual doubling of the numbers given custody between 1972 and 1982 was completely reversed by 1989. The fall in the use of custody for young offenders, and especially juveniles, was seen by reforming opinion as the one really bright spot in penal affairs in the 1980s.

It was recognised at the time that there were several reasons for what had happened. Major background factors were the steady decline of the number of teenagers in the general population throughout the period and the increased use of cautioning so that there was a considerable drop in the number of prosecutions, especially of juveniles. Another very significant factor was the development of demanding 'intermediate treatment' programmes that were belatedly being developed under the powers of the Children and Young Persons Act 1969. Magistrates became actively involved in managing the majority of these schemes, alongside people from the police, probation, education, social services and the voluntary world.

Alongside these shifts in the youth justice environment, the courts were active on the statutory sentencing criteria that had been inserted in the 1982 Act. On the ground, in the early years of the Act's operation, the confusion that Elizabeth Burney had observed seems to have shown itself in magistrates' sentencing decisions being vulnerable to appeal through lack of

[3] Burney, E., *Sentencing Young People; What Went Wrong with the Criminal Justice Act 1982* (London: Gower, 1985).

evidence that the criteria had been followed, and for a couple of years a large number of appeals to the Crown Court succeeded on those grounds. At the national level, the Court of Appeal gave authoritative rulings on the interpretation of the criteria, and some of these were encapsulated in amendments that PAPPAG prepared in order to expand and clarify the original 1982 provisions. The government accepted the PAPPAG approach, and included the revisions to the criteria as section 123 of the Criminal Justice Act 1988. In addition to expanding and clarifying the three criteria for custody, the section required any court passing a custodial sentence on a young offender to specify on which criterion it was passing the sentence and the reasons why it considered that the criterion was satisfied.

At that point the government was not prepared publicly to accept PAPPAG's further argument that the same structured sentencing criteria should be extended to adult offenders, and the clause that was moved in the House of Lords by Lord Henderson of Brompton in October 1987[4] made no headway against government opposition. As we shall see in chapter 8, however, Home Office ministers had already by that time held the first, crucial, meeting in a series during which the aim of the PAPPAG proposal would be expanded into a very much more ambitious scheme for providing a framework for principled sentencing at all levels, to be embodied in the Criminal Justice Act 1991. Meanwhile, the sentencing criteria of the 1982 Act, as revised in 1988, held the field as a prime example of reforming criminal law amendment, conceptual clarity, and effective opinion-forming close to government. Lord Windlesham saw the criteria as PAPPAG's 'greatest achievement'[5] and that is almost certainly an accurate reflection of general reforming opinion at the time.

During the second half of the 1990s, a declining number of convictions has led to a prison population that has been steadily climbing to new record levels. If one thing is clear it is that the 1991 Act's sentencing criteria, developed from the 1982 and 1988 precedents, are not effective in restraining the use of prison. It is tempting to ask, therefore, whether the 1982 and 1988 provisions ever really had much effect, or whether the reduction in the numbers of juveniles given custody in the 1980s was entirely due to the other factors that we have indicated, and to a deep shift in the thinking and feeling of sentencers about the use of custody for young people. That is probably not quite the right question. It seems clear that the provisions for recording sentencing decisions by reference to the statutory criteria at least had the effect of making magistrates think carefully about what to record, and it is perfectly feasible that the effect went deeper than that. In comparing the 1982/88 situation with that of 1991 the real point to explore is, rather,

---

[4] Hansard HL, 29 October 1987, cols 660–7.
[5] Windlesham, Lord, *Responses to Crime*, vol. 2 (Oxford: Clarendon Press, 1993).

whether the propitious circumstances of the young offender legislation were echoed for the more ambitious project. The young offender legislation was particularly important to magistrates, especially if they sat in the juvenile court, and by 1982, the previous young offender sentencing structure was universally seen as a complete mess. There was a general sense of starting afresh with a clean slate, and with a new structure that extended sentencers' powers in some aspects while restricting them in others. Against that background there seems to have been real goodwill by magistrates and their staff towards the idea of sentencing criteria, at least to the extent of being prepared to give them a try. Above all, controlling the use of custody for juveniles was an idea that went with the grain of the time, rather than cutting across it. With the benefit of hindsight it is easy to see that little or none of that kind of background was in place for the 1991 project that applied to all sentencing. It may well be that the enormously welcome reduction in the number of young people sent to custody after 1982 distracted the attention of reformers and policy-makers from the deep underlying differences between the two situations, and gave them an exaggerated idea of what could be achieved by broadly drafted sentencing criteria on their own account, simply by virtue of their statutory authority.

EARLY RELEASE

The main mechanism that provided a safety valve for the prison system during the 1980s was parole, which had been introduced by the Criminal Justice Act 1967 when Roy Jenkins was Home Secretary. Since 1940 all determinate sentences except the very shortest benefitted from one-third 'remission', so that prisoners were released automatically after two thirds of their sentence, subject to any loss of remission for disciplinary offences. Parole was to operate at any point during the middle third of a prisoner's sentence by releasing him on licence and under supervision until his normal release date. As the scheme emerged from the Parliamentary process in 1967 there were three levels of decision-making — the Home Secretary, the national Parole Board (comprised of very reputable experts including High Court judges), and the Local Review Committees (LRCs), which considered cases from the individual prison establishments. During the next 20 years there were several changes in the precise roles of the three levels and this account does not try to go into all the detail. The basic idea remained throughout that the Home Secretary was not obliged to release any prisoner on parole, and that he could not do so without the appropriate recommendation from the parole machinery.

Parole did not start with the intention of relieving pressure on the prisons: the suspended sentence, also introduced by the 1967 Act, was much more consciously focused on that role. Parole was conceived before the rehabilitative ideal had collapsed and the way it was described in the 1965 White Paper that announced the scheme is almost certainly a transparent account of what was in the minds of Home Office ministers and officials at the time, 'A considerable number of long-term prisoners reach a recognisable peak in their training at which they may respond to generous treatment, but after which, if kept in prison, they may go downhill'.[6] The other aspect that weighed with the 1960s creators of parole was public protection, and this is the right point to record that in the event it has been consistently demonstrated that prisoners released on parole have reoffended less than those released into the community 'cold'.

In its early years the parole scheme was run very cautiously, with parole only being granted to a little over 25 per cent of applicants. In 1972 the rules were changed to allow the Home Secretary to define categories of prisoners who could be released by him without reference to the main Parole Board, provided they had been unanimously recommended by the LRC, and in 1975 Roy Jenkins, again Home Secretary, encouraged the Parole Board and the LRCs to adopt a much less restrictive policy, especially with minor property offenders. By 1981 (when about 55 per cent of applications were succeeding, with over 3,000 ex-prisoners on parole licence at any one time) the scheme's capacity for reducing the prison population was certainly a major factor in the way it was viewed at the Home Office.

Under the original parole scheme there was a minimum period of 12 months' imprisonment that had to be served before parole could be considered, which meant that the shortest sentence to qualify for parole was about 20 months. This led both the Parole Board and the Home Office to ponder about the paradox that the most serious offenders could qualify for parole whilst the least serious could not, and to consider whether there was any way in which the benefits of parole could be brought to the disadvantaged prisoners serving short sentences.

The Parole Board set up a study group to explore the idea of running parole as a 'two-tier' system with truncated procedures for the lower tier, and its Annual Report for 1981 recorded that a number of members of the Board were in favour of reducing the minimum qualifying period to six months. The Home Office produced a slim document entitled *Review of Parole in England and Wales*. This discussed the possibility of extending parole to shorter-sentence prisoners, and its importance was vastly increased by a personalised foreword by the Home Secretary, William Whitelaw, expressing the hope that this section would be a helpful basis for informed discussion.

The Home Office review briefly noted the possibility of reducing the minimum qualifying period so as to bring short-sentence prisoners within the

---

[6] Home Office, *The Adult Offender* (Cmnd 2852) (London: HMSO, 1965).

parole scheme. It flatly opposed that approach, however, because the process would be so compressed that parole decisions would have to be taken on much the same information that had been available to the sentencer shortly before. That would amount to resentencing by the executive. The report argued that a simpler approach would be to release all prisoners serving between six months and three years at the one-third point, and to supervise them in the community for the middle third of the sentence. That would reduce the prison population by about 7,000, while bringing short-sentence prisoners into parole would only take about 2,000 out of the prisons.

In the event, the idea of automatic early release at the one-third point did not get off the ground, and its collapse did a good deal of political damage. An article in *The Times* claimed that it had been vehemently opposed by the judiciary and the Lord Chief Justice wrongly suspected Whitelaw of planting this in order to cover his tracks.[7] Lord Lane therefore refused to continue with the novel idea of meeting the Home Secretary to discuss matters of shared interest, and instead severed all contact with him for a period by way of punishment. Politically, the episode was a factor in Whitelaw's loss of the law and order motion at the Conservative Party conference of 1981, though the debate was a confused affair from which no clear theme emerges. A month later, on 27 November 1981, *The Times* carried a letter from Lord Justice Lawton saying that the Lord Chief Justice and other senior judges had indeed opposed the early release idea because it would have meant that persistent burglars who currently got sentences of 18 to 24 months would have been back on the street burgling again within six months.

As the Bill for the Criminal Justice Act 1982 went through Parliament, however, a campaign got under way to take the pressure off the prisons, especially the local prisons where overcrowding was concentrated. Attention switched back to the idea of reducing the minimum qualifying period for parole, notwithstanding its peremptory rejection in the Home Office's review. At the suggestion of PAPPAG the government inserted an amendment, which became section 33 of the Act, to enable the period to be reduced by statutory instrument. Lord Harris of Greenwich, who had just retired from the chairmanship of the Parole Board, unsuccessfully argued for something more specific on the grounds that 'bluntly speaking, we want urgent action to deal with an increasingly grave situation in our prisons'.[8] By that time, in short, all the pressure from every quarter was to put together some sort of way to lower the reach of the parole scheme in order to relieve prison overcrowding. On the basis of the work done by the Parole Board study group, the Home Office devised machinery for a 'quick review procedure' for short sentences, in which decisions would be taken by LRCs on the basis of truncated documentation.

---

[7] Windlesham, Lord, *Responses to Crime*, vol. 2 (see note 6).
[8] Hansard HL, 1 July 1982, col. 377.

Meanwhile, with the collapse of the more ambitious project for reducing prison numbers, Whitelaw changed his direction and secured approval for the biggest prison building programme since the nineteenth century. This was eventually expanded to deliver 21 new prisons by 1994 at a cost of about £1.2 billion. He assured the House of Commons that 'we are determined to ensure that there will be room in the prison system for every person whom the judges and magistrates decide should go there, and we will continue to do whatever is necessary for that purpose'.[9]

After the 1983 general election Whitelaw was replaced as Home Secretary by Leon Brittan, and the introduction of a reduced qualifying period for parole became caught up in the package of measures, designed to signal a harsher attitude than Whitelaw's, that Brittan prepared for announcement at the 1983 Conservative Party conference. The qualifying period was to come down to six months, allowing prisoners serving about 10 months to benefit, but this was to be balanced by some severe changes in respect of more serious offenders. Prisoners serving more than five years for offences of violence or drug trafficking were told that they would be unlikely to get parole until a few months before their release date, and those serving life sentences for some types of murder were told that they would have to serve at least 20 years.

This episode probably remains the most extreme example we have seen to date of the political technique of 'bifurcation' — increasing the severity of punishment for serious offenders as a trade-off for some concession (imaginary or, as in this case, real) towards the less serious — and it raised problems at several levels. At the level of lawfulness, Brittan's action was challenged in judicial review proceedings claiming that he had wrongly fettered his own discretion in considering future parole cases, but Brittan eventually won this on a unanimous decision in the House of Lords after split decisions in the Divisional Court and the Court of Appeal. On the broader dimension of legitimacy, however, there cannot be any real doubt that such patent political manipulation left the parole system looking distinctly short on integrity and fairness. Under the new arrangements the parole rate for short sentences climbed above 75 per cent while the rate for sentences over five years dropped below 20 per cent. This pronounced widening of the effective gap between short and long sentences was itself seen as unfair within prisons, and much resentment was caused by the empty business of going through formal parole reviews to which long-sentence prisoners remained entitled, in the knowledge that the Home Secretary had declared that he was most unlikely to authorise more than a few months' parole on the last review. In its effect on the balance of the prison population the new policy was an

---

[9] Hansard HC, 25 March 1982, col. 1122.

important staging post on the road towards much higher proportions of long-sentence prisoners during the 1980s and 90s, and by 1988 the build-up of long-sentence prisoners under the tough half of Brittan's twin-track policy had almost completely offset the reduced numbers under the other half.

It soon became apparent that, while differentials between short and long sentences were being widened, the differentials within the range of shorter sentences were being drastically eroded, There was, for example, no effective difference between a sentence of nine months and one of 18 months; in each case the prisoner would be likely to be released after six months, in the first case as of right and in the second case under parole. On top of that, time spent on remand could create bizarre effects, in some circumstances actually lengthening the time to be served after sentence. The end result of all this was that judges saw their efforts to graduate sentences in proportion to culpability as being very largely nullified, and this was particularly apparent in cases where they had tried to differentiate the punishment given to groups of co-defendants. The judges soon began to grumble about this and in 1985, after only one year of the new arrangements, the Lord Chief Justice made some strong criticisms in his annual Mansion House speech, saying that the very existence of parole should be subjected to a strenuous review.[10] The Home Office then set up yet another internal working party to review the parole scheme, but it became apparent by 1987 that this was not getting anywhere, and the Conservative election manifesto included a promise to set up a thorough review of parole.

On 16 July 1987 the new Home Secretary, Douglas Hurd, revealed that the prison population of 51,029 was 9,300 over CNA and he argued that the crowded conditions in local prisons made them more likely to result in reoffending. He announced[11] that the prison service was about to take Rollestone military camp into emergency use, and that he proposed to amend the Prison Rules to give automatic 50 per cent remission to prisoners serving 12 months and less. The last measure would relieve the prisons by about 3,500 places and it would deal with some of the anomalies troubling the courts. It was, however, an interim measure awaiting the recommendations of a review committee on parole and remission arrangements that was to be set up under the chairmanship of Lord Carlisle of Bucklow QC.

Given the glaring faults in the situation and the limitations of the committee's terms of reference, the report of the Carlisle committee,[12] published in November 1988, made a better job than might have been thought possible of establishing order and credibility in the arrangements for

---

[10] *The Times*, 10 July 1985.

[11] Hansard HC, 16 July 1987, col. 1296–8.

[12] Home Office, *The Parole System in England and Wales: Report of the Review Committee* (Cm 532) (London: HMSO, 1988).

early release. Nevertheless, the committee, which boldly declared that 'we should be aiming to send fewer people to prison', was clearly irked by its restrictive remit which prevented it from inquiring into sentencing. Had the committee been given a freer hand it would surely have proposed limitations on the flow of admissions as well as ways of expediting the release of prisoners. It concluded by saying that if the government and judiciary did not succeed in securing a reduction in sentence lengths, and the prison population were to increase under the committee's proposed scheme, then there should be a root-and-branch review of sentencing law and practice, and its interaction with early release mechanisms. In the event, most of the committee's recommendations were embodied in the Criminal Justice Act 1991, the prison population has grown at an unprecedented rate, and a review of sentencing is no closer now than it was in 1988.

The Carlisle committee had no doubt that the right approach in an ideal world would be one of 'real-time custodial sentencing' as advocated by the contemporaneous Canadian Sentencing Commission, under which the time to be served would approximate very closely to what the sentencer announced in court. That would, of course, involve a great change in sentencing practice if prisoner numbers were to be kept in any sort of connection with prison capacity. In the imperfect world in which it had to operate, and with its restricted terms of reference, the committee settled for what was practicable and recommended a cleaned-up development of the Brittan model, which addressed the worst features of excessive severity at the top end and arbitrary indulgence at the bottom end. The twin-track Brittan policy itself was to be scrapped, since it was found to be wrong in both principle and practice for short and long-sentence prisoners alike.

Accepting that without a sentencing review it would not be realistic to reduce the general scale of current early release interventions, the committee built its report round the cleverly chosen core proposition that every part of a sentence should be made to mean something, even though not all of it would be served in prison. Specifically, people serving sentences of less than 12 months were to be released after serving 50 per cent, while being subject to serve the remainder if convicted of another offence during the second half; people serving between 12 months and four years were to be subject to the same regime except that the first half of the period after release would be on licence and subject to conditions and supervision; people serving fixed sentences over four years would have a similar regime to the previous group except that release between the half and two-thirds points of the sentence would be at the discretion of the Parole Board, which would take its decisions on the basis of risk alone. (There were separate arrangements for the release of life-sentence prisoners, which are too complicated to describe here.) Remission, parole and local review committees would disappear, the lottery of effectively re-sentencing short-sentence prisoners would end, discretionary early release would only apply to long-sentence prisoners between the half and two-thirds points of their sentence, and the Home Secretary would have no role in release decisions except for lifers. Virtually all this was accepted by the government and legislated in the Criminal Justice Act 1991, with the exception that the Home Secretary's veto was preserved for fixed-term sentences over seven years.

Against the odds, then, the Carlisle committee had defused an ugly muddle and come up with a subtle network of provisions that kept the early release show on the road, while impliedly recognising that this was a second-best solution. The discretionary element was greatly limited, and as a result of the committee's criticisms some improvements were made to the procedural fairness and openness of the machinery. Even so, the scheme maintained some of the effect of the Brittan arrangements in widening sentencing differentials (i.e., making long-sentence prisoners serve more of their sentences than those serving short sentences) and this effect was to be aggravated, as we shall see, by other provisions of the 1991 Act.

Between 1984, when the Brittan twin-track policy came into operation, and 1992, when the 1991 Act brought the Carlisle reforms into effect, about 5,000 ex-prisoners were out on parole at any one time. That can certainly be seen as the prison system's safety valve while the new building programme was coming on stream, though the restrictions on parole for prisoners convicted of various serious offences were a major factor in the build-up of the long-term prison population and largely nullified the reduction in numbers at the bottom end of the sentence spectrum. The arrangements were full of anomalies and flaws, and the relief they provided was at a further hidden cost. According to David Thomas[13] it was the extension of the parole system that 'brought to an end any serious interest on the part of the judiciary in the realignment of general sentencing conventions . . . as the length of the sentence passed by the court made little difference to the time served by the offender in the vast majority of cases'. The implication of David Thomas's account is that the judges themselves would have sorted out sentencing sensibly if they had only been left in peace to do it, and we are not sure that we altogether believe that. On the other hand, it is very easy to believe that the judiciary's scepticism about government initiatives in the whole area of sentencing was strengthened by the episode. The original Home Office idea of automatic release after serving one third was plainly just too far from the nominal sentence ever to be generally acceptable.[14] The judges' confidence

---

[13] Thomas, D., 'Sentencing reform: England and Wales' in Morgan, R. and Clarkson, C. (eds), *The Politics of Sentencing Reform* (Oxford: Clarendon Press, 1995).
[14] Had it ever been implemented, automatic release at one third of short sentences would also have created anomalies similar to those produced by the downward extension of parole.

in the department's ideas must have been sapped yet further by the strange results of lowering the parole threshold,[15] and this must surely have affected the way they responded to the government's next major initiative, which was meant to affect them much more directly than anything flowing from the 1982 Act.

---

[15] It appears to have been the anomalies at the bottom end of the sentence spectrum rather than the effect of the restrictions at the top end that most worried the judges.

8 Just Deserts; the Criminal Justice Act 1991

The starting point for the whole 1991 Act project[1] was the annual stocktaking meeting that the Home Secretary, Douglas Hurd, held with his junior ministers and senior officials at Leeds Castle on 28 September 1987, two months after he had been forced to increase remission to 50 per cent for prisoners serving one year or less. The September meeting had not been intended to give special prominence to prison matters, but it was jolted by the statisticians' projection that the prison population might go as high as 70,000 by the year 2000, with some acute peaks that would be especially hard to plan for.

In the event, the prison crisis of the late 1980s came to a climax in the year after the Leeds Castle meeting. In March 1988 the Army had to be authorised to run camps for the prison service, with Hurd explaining[2] that the pressure of numbers came from more cases in the Crown court, longer sentences for offences involving violence, criminal damage and drugs, and 2,000 more inmates staying in prison due to the tighter policy on parole. Later that year, though, the numbers began to fall, and they steadily declined until 1993, well after Hurd had left the Home Office. One of the most important factors in that fall was the drop in the number of young adults

---

[1] Unless and until any of the participants choose to say more in their memoirs, all that we are likely to know about the way the Criminal Justice Act 1991 took shape within the Home Office is contained in vols 2 and 3 of Lord Windlesham's series *Responses to Crime* (Oxford: Clarendon Press, 1993, 1996) and all details of the inside story in this chapter come from that source.

[2] Hansard HC, 30 March 1988, col. 1083–5.

given custody, which we described in chapter 7. This was partly due to demographic factors, but the courts' imprisonment rate for young adults was also falling and this may have owed something to the extent to which Hurd was prepared to go in 'talking down' the population at this time. In a speech[3] on 15 January 1988, for example, Hurd said, 'Despite the statutory restrictions on the use of custody for those under 21, over 20 per cent of the young men sentenced are given a custodial sentence. This is too high.' (It is only fair to add, however, that Hurd also offered his audience the reassurance that he was continuing the policy of restricting parole for prisoners serving more than five years for violent or sexual offences.)

Paradoxically, then, by the time Hurd's successor David Waddington introduced the Criminal Justice Bill in November 1990, going out of his way to claim that it would reduce the prison population, the crisis of prisoner numbers was slowly being resolved, as the numbers declined and the accommodation from the Whitelaw building programme increased. The project that Waddington unfolded, however, went far beyond any immediate prison preoccupations. Instead, it sought to provide an enduring and principled framework that covered all areas of sentencing on a basis derived from contemporary desert theory. While the Home Office certainly hoped that the prisons would eventually benefit from properly principled sentencing, it is probably true to say that it was the ideological completeness of the project that preoccupied its framers just as much as its hoped-for effects on prison numbers. It was, in fact, an unusually theoretical and conceptualised exercise and in some ways it was flawed. Whatever its defects, however, the Act represented an unprecedented effort to establish a foundation for consistent sentencing principles and it deserved a better fate than the one that soon overtook it as a result of its own shortcomings and of a significant change in the political background.

The project was developed between September 1987 and the introduction of the legislation in November 1990 by officials and ministers working closely together, with John Patten, Minister of State at the Home Office, in immediate control of the operation. On some major issues, such as the importance of statutory sentencing criteria, the project closely reflected the thinking of the main prison reform groups.[4] Patten made a point of explaining the project to Conservative backbench members of Parliament at a series of meetings, while officials kept the judiciary informed, mainly through the Judicial Studies Board. In July 1988 the Home Office published a Green Paper, *Punishment, Custody and the Community* (Cm 424), seeking views on

---

[3] Speech to South East London Branch of the Magistrates' Association, 15 January 1988. Home Office.

[4] *Criteria for Imprisonment; the Case for Statutory Guidelines on the Use of Imprisonment for Adult Offenders* (London: Penal Affairs Consortium, 1989).

the administration of non-custodial disposals and the role of the probation service. In September 1989 — Hurd's last month at the Home Office — he held a conference at Ditchley House to review progress on the project with the Lord Chancellor, the Lord Chief Justice, the Attorney-General and officials, and after that work was put in hand on the White Paper, *Crime, Justice and Protecting the Public* (Cm 965), which was published in February 1990. The legislation that was introduced in November 1990 closely followed the White Paper.

The two central decisions that flowed from the Leeds Castle meeting were to go for statutory restrictions on the use of custody for adults, on the model of what the government had already accepted for inclusion in the forthcoming legislation on young offenders, and to reorganise non-custodial sentences under the slogan 'punishment in the community' for which Hurd's special (i.e., political) adviser Edward Bickham has been given the credit. Under its politically inspired soundbite the latter proposition was an extremely important and radical departure. Previously, non-custodial disposals (probation orders, community service orders, attendance centre orders, supervision orders) had occupied an anomalous position as 'alternatives to custody'. The probation order itself was technically not even a sentence at all. All this was impossible to disentangle from the role of the probation service and the perception that it had of itself. Probation officers, whose work had originated from the work of the Church of England Temperance Society Police Court Mission in 1876, had first been given statutory recognition in the Probation of Offenders Act 1907, which defined their role as being to 'advise, assist and befriend' the offenders placed under their supervision. The probation service continued under that guiding light, nourishing an ethos of individualised social work support of its clients that was accepted and encouraged by the Home Office. By the 1980s, however, the situation had been changed fundamentally by the collapse of the rehabilitative ideal, and the probation service was locked into a seemingly endless search for a rationale and for recognition of its specific professionalism. At the risk of parodying the debate, the question was whether a probation officer's job was to support damaged characters even at the risk of leaving them as better-adjusted criminals, or whether the task was to control offenders in the interests of public protection, to divert them from offending and to make them confront their past offending behaviour. Part of the purpose of the 1991 Act project was to come down firmly in favour of emphasising the demanding nature of community penalties, in order to increase their credibility in the eyes of sentencers and public alike.

It is one thing to say that non-custodial sentences for criminal convictions are a form of punishment, but it is something rather different to tell probation officers that their law enforcement and control functions should be seen as participating in punishment. It is plain that probation officers cannot easily accept a role as 'punishers' in the sense of being agents for the deliberate administration of suffering, and some of them may have been startled to be told by Patten[5] that 'The fact is that all probation-based disposals are already in varying degrees forms of punishment. It is bizarre to scratch around to find polite euphemisms for what is going on.' The 1988 Green Paper, *Punishment, Custody and the Community*, went on to make it clear that punishment and control were the purposes of non-custodial disposals by the courts and that if the probation service refused to see its function in those terms, the government would be prepared to set up a new service to take on the role, perhaps by contracting with all the most appropriate providers, which would include, but not be limited to, the probation service. In the event the particular argument about semantics ended with most probation officers accepting that they had a control function, whatever else the government wanted to call it, and that there was too much evidence for comfort about inconsistencies and gaps in the supervision of offenders. The proper role of the probation service has, however, remained a live issue.

Despite its obvious nakedly political element, however, the idea of 'punishment in the community' went much deeper than being a slogan under which non-custodial sentences could be sold to the public and to sentencers, and under which the government could confront the probation service. It provided the framework on which much of the 1991 Act was constructed. Once it was accepted that graduated loss of liberty was the connecting thread between imprisonment, the various non-custodial disposals and, by extension, fines, then it was possible to build a single conceptual 'just deserts' framework within which all these forms of sentencing could be accommodated and made subject to consistent criteria.[6] In that way, the idea of statutory sentencing criteria and the idea of 'punishment in the community' fused together to form a genuinely robust core concept.

The 1990 White Paper presented itself as offering 'a coherent legislative framework for sentencing with the severity of the punishment matching the seriousness of the crime and a sharper distinction in the way the courts deal with violent and non-violent crimes'. For violent and sexual offences the Crown Court should have new powers to pass longer sentences if that was necessary to protect the public from serious harm. For other kinds of crime, however, the White Paper sets out an exceptionally clearly written statement of the reasons for restraint in the use of imprisonment, which it famously

---

[5] Speech to Annual Conference of Association of Chief Officers of Probation, 15 September 1988. Home Office.
[6] The formulation of a desert model for non-custodial disposals was due to Wasik and Von Hirsch in 'Non-custodial penalties and the principles of desert', *Criminal Law Review*, p. 555 (1988), which is known to have influenced the framers of the 1991 legislation.

said 'can be an expensive way of making bad people worse'. The reasons for scepticism about deterrence and rehabilitation as rationales for imprisonment are clearly set out, and it is stated that 'injustice is more likely if the courts do not focus on the seriousness of the offence before them'. At several points the White Paper stresses that punishment in the community should be an effective way of dealing with much crime and it offers courts the flexible option of choosing various permutations of community sentence in combination. The suspended sentence of imprisonment did not fit into the logical structure being proposed and it was to be limited to cases where there were good reasons against immediate imprisonment. Fines are given their place in the White Paper's coherent new system, ranking below community sentences because they involve less interference with liberty. The use of fines had, however, fallen substantially and, in order to improve enforcement and to increase sentencers' confidence in fines as a punishment by ensuring equality of impact, the government would introduce a system of means-related or 'unit' fines in magistrates' courts. All this is presented quite specifically as representing the principle of 'just deserts', which the White Paper describes as attracting increasing interest in jurisdictions such as Australia, Canada and the USA.[7] As for the way in which all this agenda should be taken forward, the White Paper carefully distinguishes between decisions in individual cases, which should never be subject to government influence, and 'sentencing principles and sentencing practice' which 'are matters of legitimate concern to government'. The White Paper makes it clear that what it envisages is a partnership between Parliament and the courts, in which Parliament would lay down the basic framework of core sentencing principles, within which the Court of Appeal would develop detailed principles and guidance.

The Bill translated the White Paper project into a basic structure like that of a pyramid, with the criteria for custody at the apex and with the criteria for lesser sentences ranked below. Subject to provisions about multiple offences discussed below, custody could be given only if the offence was so serious that only such a sentence was justified or, where the offence was a violent or sexual one, only if such a sentence would be adequate to protect the public from serious harm from the offender. Parallel provisions then required the court to pass a sentence of a term that was commensurate with the seriousness of the offence, or of such longer term as was necessary to protect the public. A similar set of provisions controlled community sentences, with an initial test of seriousness of the offence, and a provision that the restriction of liberty imposed by the court should also be commensurate with

---

[7] The commendatory reference to the USA is puzzling in a document as late as 1990. By that time the history of determinate sentencing, desert theory and an exploding prison population in the USA was evident.

seriousness. In the case of community sentences there was an additional provision that the court should make orders that were most suitable for the offender. Thus, the aim of rehabilitation is excluded from the sentencer's consideration in the case of imprisonment, but is allowed to influence the choice of community sentences . Fines should simply reflect the seriousness of the offence, but were subject to a complex means-related procedure in magistrates' courts.

It will be seen that the Bill developed the White Paper's proposals on violent and sex offenders into the specific provision that they should be liable, on public protection grounds, to longer sentences (within the statutory maximum) than is warranted by the seriousness of their offence. This is straightforward preventive incapacitation rather than just deserts, and the Bill lacked any suggestion of the need for procedural safeguards in these cases, such as a requirement for medical evidence. This incapacitation element appears to have been mainly due to Waddington and it constitutes another major landmark on the way to a deliberate policy of bifurcation. It is very obtrusive on the face of the legislation, especially since the rival principle of just deserts is never stated directly and is left to be supported entirely by the references to the criterion of seriousness of the offence that are scattered throughout. A great deal would evidently depend on the interpretation of the word 'seriousness' and there are other aspects on which the Bill was tentative; for example, no ranking order between the different kinds of community sentence was suggested, and the courts were left to decide for themselves how the different types of order compared with each other in the restriction of liberty. In broad terms, though, the project can be seen as a carefully balanced package with a general thrust that is hard to fault. The points on which the project became politically discredited in 1993 — the detailed specifics of the unit fine regime, and the treatment of previous convictions and multiple offences — were not fundamental to the main structure.

Even without the addition of the provision for longer sentences on public protection grounds, the project lent itself to being presented and perceived as tough or liberal, according to the audience. Thus Hurd told the Conservative Party conference in October 1989 that the sentencing system had become muddled and had lost public confidence; the proposals he was preparing would have the plain guiding principle that every 'convicted criminal should receive his just deserts in the severity and length of his sentence'. The conference gave a good reception to this but it is rather unlikely that this particular audience had quite the same view of 'just deserts' that the White Paper had. When the White Paper was published on 7 February 1990 *The Times* commented in a leader that if the penal pendulum was not to swing too far and fast the government would need to pay more attention to the offender, rather than to retribution. Because the project mainly dealt with abstract principles and left the question of what constituted 'seriousness' hanging in the air, outside observers could read into it what they wished. This ambivalence was accentuated by the Bill's gnomic drafting. We do not think that the trouble with the components that went wrong can simply be blamed on the drafter, however. There seems to have been a much deeper ambiguity in the government's[8] approach, especially regarding the treatment of previous convictions. This was a high-profile issue right from the start, and we must describe it fully. The next few paragraphs inevitably have to go into rather a lot of detail.

The treatment of previous convictions is one of the basic sentencing questions. The approach approved by the Court of Appeal in several judgments has been labelled 'progressive loss of mitigation'; that is, the sentencer should first decide the ceiling that is warranted by the seriousness of the current offence and then consider what, if any, discount is justified on grounds of a good record or any other factors. A clean record can earn a significant discount, unless the offence is a very serious one such as rape, but the discount is progressively used up by successive convictions. An offender with a really bad record is left with no discount and should be sentenced at the ceiling. The case of *Queen*[9] sets out this principle and was cited by the 1990 White Paper in support of the proposition that the seriousness of the current offence should be 'the primary factor in sentencing' while 'a good record may enable the court to reduce the sentence'. How far courts actually accepted *Queen* or the principle it articulates appears to be doubtful:[10] while several Court of Appeal judgments took the same line as Queen, there were also others that did not. The practical application of the principle is that if an offence, typically theft, is too minor to warrant imprisonment then offenders should not go to prison, however bad their previous record. Some sentencers have never accepted that, and send persistent minor property offenders to prison. That approach is called 'sentencing on record'.

If the government had clearly stated at any time during the passage of the legislation that it stood by the *Queen* principle all might have been well. It never did so. The whole question of previous convictions had become a lively issue among desert theorists at that time and many of them thought that previous convictions should be largely disregarded, with nothing more than a modest discount for a first offender.[11]

---

[8] We use 'government' as a neutral word simply to denote the line taken by government spokesmen, without any implications concerning the internal processes of policy formulation and approval.

[9] (1981) 3 Cr App R (S) 245.

[10] Ashworth, A., *Sentencing and Criminal Justice* (London: Butterworths, 1995), pp. 157–8.

[11] Von Hirsch, A., *Past or Future Crimes; Deservedness and Dangerousness in the Sentencing of Criminals* (Manchester: Manchester University Press, 1986).

We know from Lord Windlesham's account that Home Office officials showed the senior judges on the Judicial Studies Board some draft clauses for the Bill and that the judges were unhappy both on this issue and on the treatment of multiple offences. We do not know exactly what happened, but on 4 September 1990 *The Times* carried an article saying that the judiciary had forced the Home Office to think again about its proposal that previous convictions should be ignored. On 16 October Waddington held a press conference at which this issue was one of the main points of interest. The line that Waddington took sounded very much like support for 'sentencing on record' since he said: 'If a fellow has committed an offence which is near the top of the range for community service, near the breaking point where the person might go to prison, then it's quite difficult to argue against the proposition that as it is the second or third offence that person should go to jail'.[12]

When the Bill was published on 9 November 1990 it was found to deal with previous convictions in a novel and confusing way that was quite different from that which Waddington had trailed. In the provisions on custodial sentences it was first laid down that an offence was not to be regarded as more serious by reason of any previous convictions but then there was a provision that enabled a court to take the *circumstances* of previous offences into account if they were relevant. The government was tested on the point in both the Commons and the Lords, and the relevant provision was modified in the Lords. It eventually became section 29, which allowed courts to take account of aggravating factors disclosed by the circumstances of previous offences, while mitigation was covered by another new provision (section 28) which enabled a court to mitigate a sentence by virtue of any matter that it considered relevant. The reason for that provision was that the Bill as introduced had arguably prevented courts from taking into account any mitigating factors that did not arise from the current offence, which would have been a revolutionary change that the government disavowed as being its intention. All this was highly confusing, and the kind of circumstances that made an offence more serious never really emerged from the mist, though racially motivated attacks and shopkeepers selling bad food were quoted as examples of a persistent pattern of behaviour. Nevertheless, although the government never managed to say so forthrightly, the Act in its final form made it possible for the courts to operate the *Queen* principle of progressive loss of mitigation, since section 29 prevented courts from sentencing more heavily than was warranted by the seriousness of the current offence, while section 28 enabled mitigation on account of any matter, which must include the cleanness of the offender's previous criminal record. There

---

[12] *The Times*, 17 October 1990.

still remained, however, the curious extra provision in section 29 that in deciding on the seriousness of an offence the court could take into account any aggravating factors that were disclosed by the circumstances of previous offences (if, that is, it was able to discover them).

It is tempting to speculate how this confusing state of affairs came about, though the important thing is the end-product rather than the route taken to arrive at it. For our part, we do not think that it is right to shoot the pianist (in this case the drafter), since we think that the format of first disallowing reference to previous convictions and then enabling reference to their circumstances is so unusual that it must have had strong roots in the instructions that were given. Neither do we think that the government's initial intention could have been simply to endorse *Queen*. If that had been the case, it would have been a simple matter to say so. Our guess is that at some stage in the policy's formulation the framers of the Bill were attracted by a purist just deserts approach that would have made the seriousness of the current offence the *only* consideration (and which, incidentally, might have limited the possibility of mitigating for a good record) and then at some later stage the provision to enable 'circumstances' of previous offences to be taken into account was added as a compromise counterweight in order to toughen the policy. The result was that both elements remained, despite being in conflict with each other. The pattern has some similarity to the addition of incapacitatory public protection sentences to the basic just deserts model. Be all that as it may, the legislation reached the statute book with its intentions on the treatment of previous convictions still regarded as something of a riddle. For example, an authoritative manual on the Act that was produced at the time for the use of practitioners commented, 'This is an area of some complexity, as to which readers who require additional commentary are referred to [a specialist legal companion volume]'.[13]

A similar basic question in sentencing is the treatment of multiple offences (i.e., several convictions that are up for sentence at the same time). The Bill's approach to this echoed the way in which it tackled previous convictions, and was destined to lead to the same repudiation in 1993. The courts' general approach to multiple convictions is to apply the principle of 'totality', which is an imprecise view that the overall sentence should be proportionate both to the totality of offending and to the scale of sentencing for other kinds of offence. The 1988 Act's amendments to the sentencing criteria for young offenders, however, had stipulated that custody should be used only if an offence was 'so serious that a non-custodial sentence for it cannot be justified'. The Court of Appeal eventually held[14] that the phrase 'for it' must

---

[13] Ashworth, A., Cavadino, P., Rutherford, A. et al., *Introduction to the Criminal Justice Act 1991* (Winchester: Waterside, 1992).

[14] In *Davison* (1989) 11 Cr App R (S) 570.

mean that if a defendant was due to be sentenced on several counts at the same time, the sentencing court should consider them individually and could not give a custodial sentence if none of the individual offences was sufficiently serious to warrant it. This approach was considered by the framers of the 1991 Bill to be right on merits, since they feared that sentencing courts might give custodial sentences for several minor current offences taken together, in just the same way that they might 'sentence on record' because of previous convictions. The draft clauses that were shown to senior judges therefore spelt it out that the various 'seriousness' tests in the Bill had to be satisfied in respect of a single offence, no matter how many were being dealt with on the same occasion. The judges disliked this and Lord Justice Glidewell led a deputation to try to persuade Waddington to change his mind. All that Waddington was prepared to concede, however, was the awkward and arbitrary compromise that one other offence (making two in all) could be taken into account, and the Bill went ahead on that basis.

Once again, the point was probed in the Commons and the Lords. In particular, Lord Ackner, a Law Lord speaking after consultation with the Lord Chief Justice,[15] put down amendments on the Bill's third reading including one that would have enabled courts to apply the seriousness test to a series of similar offences taken together. Ackner gave the example of a person who stole £100 a week from his employer over a long period, who would escape custody if the seriousness test had to be limited to only 2 counts but who would deserve to be imprisoned for the overall scale of his crime, and he made it clear that he regarded the Bill as also being unrealistically restrictive in its approach to previous convictions and response to previous sentences.[16] His description of just deserts as a 'platitudinous policy' can now be seen as a sufficiently clear indication of the senior judiciary's attitude, though it is unlikely that its full implications were hoisted on board at the time. Be that as it may, the government preferred its own amendments that enabled courts to take the circumstances of multiple (as well as previous) offences into account as aggravating factors. Ackner's amendment was negatived, as was his subsequent one on response to previous sentences.

---

[15] Windlesham, Lord, *Responses to Crime* vol. 3. But it is not clear that the Lord Chief Justice's involvement was made known at the time.

[16] In addition to limiting the way in which previous convictions could be taken into account, the 1991 legislation also prevented courts from regarding an offender's response to previous sentences as an aggravating factor. This reversed the 1982 Act's provision for young offenders that had been revised and improved only three years previously in the 1988 Act. Lord Ackner attacked this in the Lords committee stage of the 1991 Act on 18 April 1991, saying that it 'just does not make sense'. The Home Office minister Lord Ferrers told him that the 1988 Act's provision was 'a form of sentencing on record which we consider undesirable. Community penalties are penalties in their own right. We feel that once the punishment has been completed the offender should not be in jeopardy again for the earlier offence.' (Hansard HL, 18 April 1991, col. 1621–2.)

The third element that was to collapse in 1993 was the means-related system for fines in magistrates' courts, and this attracted no real questions when the 1991 Act was going through Parliament. Basically, the scheme required magistrates' courts to set the seriousness level of the offence in terms of units and then to attach a value to the units by reference to the defendant's disposable income, measured by a prescribed means assessment. The scheme was rigid and prescriptive as to detail but it had been satisfactorily piloted in four court areas by the Home Office. What changed between the pilots and the 1991 legislation was the government's decision to increase the level of fines and, with it, the maximum value of a unit, which had been in the £25 to £35 range for the pilots but was raised to £100 by the 1991 Act. Although the implications of this were not spotted at the time, they became apparent well before the Act came into force in October 1992. A commentary on the Act,[17] that was produced in 1992, for example, said 'Whilst an increase in maximum fine levels was overdue, the raising of the maximum levels by a factor of two and a half, and during an unprecedented economic recession, at the same time as the introduction of unit fines themselves — with the accompanying culture shock — has led to criticism of unit fines generally'.

We are looking at the 1991 legislation with the benefit of hindsight and it is important not to get the points that went wrong out of perspective. Labour opposed the Bill's second reading but on grounds that had nothing to do with the points we have mentioned. The main Labour argument was that the Bill was inadequate and that it ignored the need for such things as a code of prison standards and a sentencing council (which was eventually considered and voted down in the Lords). The other things that attracted most Parliamentary interest were, in the Commons, the provisions for private prison services and, in the Lords, the abolition of the mandatory life sentence for murder which had a big majority in the Lords but which was reversed by the Commons. Nevertheless, concern about the flaws in the Act was never far below the surface. Even such an enthusiast for the main principles of the Bill as Lord Windlesham was gloomy when he made his final speech on its third reading in the Lords. What he said was:

> I still have great problems with the Bill, particularly as regards the ambivalence that still exists towards the treatment of previous convictions and towards offences being taken into consideration. I also believe that the definition of seriousness and serious harm will cause problems for the courts. It would be over optimistic to expect any sudden or dramatic fall in the size of the prison population.[18]

---

[17] Ashworth, A. et al., *Materials on the Criminal Justice Act 1991* (Winchester: Waterside, 1992).

[18] Hansard HL, 4 June 1991, col. 637.

Between July 1991, when the Act was given Royal Assent, and October 1992, when it entered into force, the Home Office carried out an extensive programme of briefing meetings, conferences and training for the criminal justice practitioners who would be affected by it. At the same time the Judicial Studies Board carried out its own parallel information exercise for the judges. There has long been some suspicion that these two exercises were of very different kinds, and light was cast on this by Lord Thomas of Gresford during the debates on the Crime (Sentences) Bill in 1997. What Lord Thomas then said[19] was:

> Nobody could understand why suddenly, contrary to the whole history of the criminal justice system in this country, a person's past record was to be ignored. At sentencing conferences we were informed that that was because there were not enough prison places and that it was our duty, according to the Home Office, to reduce the prison population, to which . . . a very senior judge replied, 'Now listen boys, if you want to send them to prison, if you think that that is what should be done, you send them to prison'. That was quite contrary to the advice that was given to us by the Home Office at that time.

This was a period when profound changes were taking place in the political environment. In March 1992 record increases in recorded crime were announced for the second year running, the increases being concentrated in property crime and, we would say, reflecting the ongoing deep economic recession that was influenced by the country's participation in the European Exchange Rate Mechanism (ERM) at too high a parity. In April the Major administration was re-elected at the general election and the House of Commons changed considerably in its composition and mood, so that John Patten's briefing of backbench Conservatives in 1988 became less relevant. Kenneth Clarke was appointed Home Secretary — the third since Douglas Hurd, under whom the original ideas for the 1991 Act had been put together. In May the government introduced the European Communities (Amendment) Bill to enable the United Kingdom to ratify the Treaty on European Union that had been concluded at Maastricht the previous December, and it was soon clear that the 'Eurosceptic' Conservative backbenchers in the Commons were going to give the government a difficult time in getting the legislation through Parliament. Those difficulties were compounded when the Maastricht Treaty was repudiated by a constitutional referendum in Denmark. On 16 September the United Kingdom was forced to leave the ERM, and the government's economic policy collapsed. The Commons were recalled for

---

[19] Hansard HL, 13 February 1997, col. 430.

an emergency debate and the government's rating in the public opinion polls plummeted catastrophically (never to recover, as it turned out).

On 29 September 1992 Lord Taylor of Gosforth, the new Lord Chief Justice, gave a press conference at which he was asked about the 1991 Act, which was coming into force the following month. Anyone listening, and especially anyone who was familiar with the tensions within the Act, must have had a sense of foreboding on hearing Lord Taylor say, 'Not only judges, but the public, will have some misgivings about a regime in which the previous record and number of offences committed are minimised to the extent which this Act does'.[20] At that time, though, nobody could have foreseen quite how the problems of the Act would interact with the changed political scene to bring about the convulsion of the following year.

---

[20] *The Times*, 30 September 1992.

9 The Watershed

For two decades after the Second World War law and order had hardly figured as a party political issue, and the public and media attitude to criminal justice policy seems, by modern standards, to have been almost unbelievably respectful, as though the awe that still surrounded the judicial process was in some sense extended to discussion of the underlying policy issues. The first signs of change were in the 1960s, when both the Labour and Conservative parties began to give increased space to law and order in their election manifestos, without suggesting that crime was the direct consequence of the policies of the other party. That mould was broken in the 1970 general election, when the Conservative manifesto argued that the Labour government 'cannot entirely shrug off responsibility' for the rise in crime and violence, and asserted that the law needed to be made more effective 'for dealing with offences . . . peculiar to the age of demonstration and disruption'. That linkage between, on the one hand, crime and, on the other hand, industrial dispute and civil protest stimulated the complaint in the Labour manifesto that 'nothing could be more cynical than the current attempts of our opponents to exploit for party political ends the issue of crime and law enforcement'.

Throughout the 1970s the Conservative Party continued to cast itself as the traditional upholder of equality under the law, in contrast to the Labour Party, which was implied to be selective in its view of the law, at least in the context of industrial relations. Labour's response was to say as little as possible on the issue, and this proved no barrier to its winning both the general elections of 1974. By the 1979 election, however, a clearly polarised situation had developed that was to prove profoundly influential right up to the 1997 election and, it seems, beyond. Labour's 1979 manifesto focused on dealing with crime through its social and economic programme for tackling inequality, poverty and deprivation. The Conservative manifesto, in contrast, raised the profile of law and order to rank as one of the party's five major tasks. It specifically accused Labour of having undermined the rule of law, and set out a list of undertakings including 'tough sentences . . . for violent criminals and thugs' and the 'short, sharp shock' regime for young offenders mentioned in chapter 7. This finally marked the end of the post-Second World War consensus approach to law and order in British politics, and the Conservative Party had every reason to believe that it was electorally effective to a remarkable degree. MORI polls showed the Conservative lead over Labour on law and order to be 30 percentage points, and none of the other issues tested by MORI between August 1978 and April 1979 came anywhere near that.[1] Furthermore, the growth in Conservative support during the general election period was greater for law and order than for any other issue.

During the 1980s the Conservative Party maintained a comfortable lead over Labour on law and order, though the issue was not very prominent in either of the general elections of 1983 and 1986. Both parties agreed about the importance of victim support and both subscribed to the general theory that serious violent criminals should be given long sentences of imprisonment while the less serious (rarely defined sufficiently clearly to be recognisable) should be diverted into a better range of non-custodial disposals. The important differences between the parties lay more in the discourse about the connection, or lack of it, between crime and wider social conditions. For the Conservatives, individual accountability, and the effective exercise of authority by family and school, was paramount. For Labour, crime bred in conditions of poverty, deprivation and disadvantage, and it could only be brought under control when these deep ills in society had been tackled.

The parties continued to occupy these respective territories up to the 1992 general election, though concern about crime was increased by the unparalleled rise in recorded crime by nearly 40 per cent in the two years 1990 and 1991, with the figures for the latter year released immediately before the election period. During 1991 there were also lurid press accounts of a crime wave among young people, especially taking the form of joyriding and 'hotting' stolen cars, and a long campaign by the press and some police forces to draw attention to the number of offences committed by people on bail and to the activities of allegedly high-offending juveniles. Against all that background the Conservatives may not have had much incentive to draw attention to law and order in the campaign, though two months before the

---

[1] Butler, D. and Kavanagh, D., *The British General Election of 1979* (London: Macmillan, 1980).

election they produced a poster showing a policeman with one arm tied behind his back, with the caption 'Labour's soft on crime'. Labour, for its part, rested on an approach to crime through social policies, while arguing for an increase in police numbers, and it did not do anything significant to draw attention to law and order issues throughout the campaign. Once again, the election passed off with very little said on the issue and with the Conservatives generally reckoned to have remained in comfortable occupation of this territory. Following Labour's defeat in the election John Smith succeeded Neil Kinnock as leader and Tony Blair took over from Roy Hattersley as shadow Home Secretary.

At the time of the United Kingdom's enforced departure from the ERM in September 1992 the main crime concern continued to be the alleged crime wave among young people, with the particular spectre of persistent offending by children too young to be made subject to any form of custodial court order then available. The Home Secretary, Kenneth Clarke, proposed in October that a new kind of custodial provision should be established for these young people and during the following months the topic remained in the public eye as the Home Affairs Committee of the House of Commons set up an inquiry about it and the bodies submitting evidence to it lobbied publicly for support. (In the event, this new kind of custodial regime became the secure training order for children aged 12 to 14 which was included in the Criminal Justice and Public Order Act 1994.) The last couple of months of 1992 also saw the beginning of critical media coverage of the 1991 Act.

It was against that background that Tony Blair completely repositioned the Labour Party on crime and punishment during the course of an interview on BBC Radio 4's 'The World This Weekend' on 10 January 1993. He began with the famous slogan that he was to use repeatedly from then on and which was to feature four times in the 1997 Labour manifesto, saying, 'I think it's important that we are tough on crime and tough on the causes of crime too'. After giving examples of antisocial behaviour that should 'be punished, if necessary severely' he explained that 'There's the side of personal responsibility, which we must enforce against those that are committing crime, but then there's also some of the deeper and underlying causes, which we've also got to address'. He easily avoided the charge of trying to have his cake and eat it by arguing that 'Society, if you like, has not merely a duty, it is in its interest, to try and create the conditions in which people get a chance in life. But the other side of that, and this is maybe where the left-of-centre parties have not faced up to things the way they should, is: where people are given chances, they're expected to take them, and they're expected to take responsibility for their own individual actions.' Questioned on his attitude to locking up children of 12 as some of the police were currently advocating, he acknowledged that 'The reoffending rate for those that then come out of these institutions is very, very high' and argued that it was best 'to intervene at a much earlier stage with penalties and punishments within the community'.

Finally, on his attitude to the size of the prison population, he said, 'You've got to be prepared to punish . . . and, where necessary, that will mean custody. But let's be quite clear, the objective of any sensible Home Secretary is not to increase the prison population . . . you've got to try to deal with both aspects of this problem.'

This was a deft handling of an issue that had plagued the Labour Party since at least 1979. It was, in fact, such an obvious political position waiting to be scooped up that it is surprising that this had not happened before. We shall be going on to argue that it is still not clear how the Labour government proposes to interpret each half of the famous soundbite in practice. Be that as it may, in 1993 the Labour Party leapt free with one bound from the shackles that had weighed it down, and the general perception that this had happened must have been a major factor in the way that matters subsequently developed.

The following month, on 12 February 1993, there occurred the one terrible event in this story that still reverberates in the country's memory. Two-year-old Jamie Bulger was abducted from a busy Liverpool shopping centre, led through the streets for two and a half miles to a railway line, and was there battered to death with bricks and an iron bar. It was every parent's nightmare and it was brought vividly into every household in the country by the poignant image from a security video camera showing the trusting child hand in hand with one of his abductors. During the next few days the media carried harrowing stories of the child's last journey through the streets and the initial shock of the event settled into a public mood of vengeful hatred, puzzled introspection and fear of crime that seemed able to strike at will, even in the most everyday and public situation. It was more than a week before it became clear that Jamie's two murderers were ten-year-old children: by that time the public attitude was fixed and the case had built up a huge symbolic charge that somehow needed to be released. It was, in fact, a genuine example of moral panic on a national scale, and there was virtually no media or political comment pointing out that murder by young children is a very rare phenomenon that occurs in all countries, and that it is hard to think of a more atypical kind of offence, or one from which it is less possible to draw general lessons. Instead, the political response urged soul-searching and a change of course, albeit with characteristically different tones of voice.

On 19 February Tony Blair made a widely reported speech at Wellingborough in which he said, 'The news bulletins of the last week have been like hammer-blows struck against the sleeping conscience of the country. . . . We cannot exist in a moral vacuum. If we do not learn and then teach the value of what is right and what is wrong, then the result is simply moral chaos which engulfs us all.'[2]

On 20 February Kenneth Clarke put out a brusque statement urging Parliament to 'catch up with the mood of the people' on crime, and to 'spend more time condemning criminals and less producing mealy-mouthed excuses for them'.[3]

On 21 February the *Mail on Sunday* carried a full centre-spread interview with John Major by the newspaper's editor, Jonathan Holborrow. The opening words were 'It had been a terrible week, not just for the man himself but for the country. . . . New records of unemployment had shocked the nation, while in the Commons the seemingly endless internecine strife with the Maastricht rebels continued, and a series of brutal crimes horrified Britain.' Major then developed a line that was extremely similar to Blair's Wellingborough speech, but with the addition of frequent references to the need for condemnation, as had been trailed by Clarke the previous day. 'There is a distinction between right and wrong. You know whether what you are doing is right or wrong and other people know it as well. I think the public generally need to draw that distinction in the case of people who are guilty of wrongdoing. That is why I believe they should condemn. If they do not condemn they may appear to approve tacitly.' The interview concluded with Major saying that his concern was to be considerate to victims rather than to criminals, and that he 'would like a crusade against crime'. The whole article appeared under the banner headline 'Major on criminals: we should condemn a little more, understand a little less'.

The collapse of the government's confidence, the new credibility of the Labour Party, the swollen crime figures and the law and order tone of much of the media had all conspired to encourage an attack on crime as a unifying theme to distract attention from the government's difficulties. That was the febrile background against which the fate of the 1991 Act was settled.

When the 1991 Act was brought into force on 1 October 1992 it was the unit fine provisions that initially attracted public criticism, since they immediately ran into a press campaign that did not acknowledge the rationale of equal impact between offenders of different means, and criticised different fines for similar offences committed by rich and poor individuals as though they were grotesque aberrations, rather than the result that the legislation had been intended to achieve. It soon became clear, however, that the sheer size of the increase in fines for better-off offenders was taking everyone, including many magistrates, by surprise, and that there was a particular anomaly in the disproportion between such fines for motoring offences and the very much lower fixed penalties for the same offences. Soon, it also became apparent

---

[2] Rentoul, J., *Tony Blair* (London: Warner Books, 1995).
[3] *Sunday Times*, 21 February 1993.

that there were problems in operating the means assessment regime stipulated in the Act, and that where defendants failed to supply information about their means many courts were setting fines at the maximum income level simply as a sanction to impel them to provide the information. This technique led to absurd cases such as the notorious one of the man from Cwmbran who was initially fined £1,200 for dropping a crisp packet from his car. The press had a field day with all these embarrassments, and there was a genuine feeling among many magistrates that the prescriptive nature of the scheme together with the high maximum value that the Act attached to units was preventing them from doing justice. By 4 May 1993 the scheme was in serious trouble and Kenneth Clarke suggested to a deputation from the Magistrates' Association that a compromise solution might be to enable courts to review the final cash figure resulting from the Act's system of calculations, before confirming it as the fine to be imposed. That day a bulletin was sent to all branches of the Magistrates' Association encouraging them to make maximum use of their existing discretion, but this was repudiated next day by the Justices' Clerks' Society who saw it as unwarranted interference with the judicial process (a matter for the detection of which the society has a famously well-developed flair).[4] A further meeting between officials and the Magistrates' Association was arranged for 12 May, but this was cancelled at short notice and Kenneth Clarke told the House of Commons the next day that the unit fine scheme would be abolished entirely — a decision that left the chairman of the Magistrates' Association 'absolutely amazed'.[5]

Meanwhile, serious developments had been taking place on the interpretation of the Act's provisions on custodial sentencing, described in chapter 8. During the last week of November 1992 the Court of Appeal led by Lord Taylor heard nine appeals that served to illustrate various aspects of the new legislation, on which the Court gave carefully reasoned judgments. For our purposes the only significant ones are those discussed in the next three paragraphs.

The importance of *Cunningham*[6] is that it established deterrence as an objective of sentencing, notwithstanding the 1990 White Paper's statement that the aim of the reforms was to establish 'a new legislative framework for sentencing, based on the seriousness of the offence or just deserts', and the incompatibility of deterrence reasoning with 'just deserts' theory. For all the reasons canvassed at various points in this book, there simply is no sound reason for believing that general deterrent results can be obtained by

---

[4] Windlesham, Lord, *Responses to Crime*, vol. 3 (Oxford: Clarendon Press, 1996).

[5] Cavadino, M. and Dignan, J., *The Penal System; an Introduction*, 2nd ed. (London: Sage, 1997).

[6] (1993) 14 Cr App R (S) 444.

adjustments of sentencing within the limits that exist in practice. Nevertheless, judges are deeply and genuinely attached to the idea of deterrence, as one can verify any day by looking at a few trial reports in the newspapers. The 1990 White Paper carefully explained the fragility of assuming deterrent effects and walked all round the subject without actually saying in black and white that deterrence should no longer be considered a proper aim of sentencing. The Act itself simply stated in section 2(2)(a) that 'The custodial sentence shall be for such term . . . as in the opinion of the court is commensurate with the seriousness of the offence' so that the single word 'seriousness' had to do all the work. In these circumstances Lord Taylor had no problem in deciding that:

> The purposes of a custodial sentence must primarily be to punish and to deter. Accordingly the phrase 'commensurate with the seriousness of the offence' must mean commensurate with the punishment and deterrence which the seriousness of the offence requires.

Having accepted deterrence as a valid criterion, Lord Taylor moved on to include the associated justification of prevalence as well, arguing that if a type of offence was prevalent in an area then the sentence commensurate with seriousness might need to be higher there than elsewhere. The reasoning for this rested on the proposition that each offence of a prevalent type affected not only the immediate victim but all those in the area who were put in fear, but nothing was said about the well-known difficulty of establishing whether a particular type of offence is, in fact, prevalent or not. The one limitation that Lord Taylor did recognise was that section 2(2)(a) prohibited increasing a sentence simply to make an example of a particular offender.

The *Cunningham* judgment went a very long way to rip the conceptual heart out of the Act, since it left sentencers free to take their choice from a 'cafeteria' menu of proportionality and deterrence, with a booster available for prevalence (and with incapacitation also available under the Act for sexual and violent offences). That did not necessarily mean that the Court of Appeal disabled itself from developing more comprehensive sentencing guidance that could broadly be described as promoting consistency, but it did mean that any dreams of a single unifying criterion could be discarded within weeks of the Act coming into force.

In *Bexley*[7] the Court of Appeal considered the question of previous convictions. Lord Taylor recognised that sentencing on record had been prevalent when he noted that the new Act forbade 'the approach, commonly

---

[7] (1993) 14 Cr App R (S) 462.

adopted before the Act, of regarding the instant offence as more serious and deserving of custody because it repeated previous offences which had been treated more leniently'. He made it clear that it was already an established principle that 'an offender who has been punished for offences committed in the past should not in effect be punished for them again' and that the Act merely restated that principle. In the case of *Cox*[8] he decided that the defendant's light criminal record justified a non custodial sentence even though the current offence was serious enough to justify custody. Taken together, *Bexley* and *Cox* therefore established that the 1991 Act simply embodied the principle established by *Queen* and other leading cases, that is, the sentencing ceiling for the current offence should be set by its seriousness, but there could be mitigation for a good record. As for the 1991 Act's additional component of the 'circumstances' of previous offences, Lord Taylor gave an impeccable ruling that the sentencer should first consider the seriousness of the current offence and then consider whether there were circumstances of previous offences that cast light on it, so as to disclose some aggravating factor.

As had been predicted during the 1991 Act's Parliamentary passage, the courts ran into practical difficulties in finding out about the 'circumstances' of previous offences, since this often implied a greater degree of detail about previous convictions than was readily available. The complaints by judges and magistrates, however, were not so much about that point as about the general idea that the new Act prevented them from taking previous convictions into account. The correct answer to that was that the Court of Appeal had made it clear in *Bexley* and *Cox* that the new Act merely restated the old principle of *Queen*, but nobody seems to have given that answer. Instead, in a speech[9] to the Law Society of Scotland at Gleneagles on 21 March 1993, Lord Taylor launched a bitter attack on the 1991 Act generally, and these provisions in particular, claiming that the Act was 'forcing the judge into an ill-fitting straitjacket'.

The main thrust of the Gleneagles speech was to make an unqualified claim to total judicial discretion, and to repel all boarders. Thus, 'The court needs to have available the widest range of possible measures, and the broadest discretion to deploy them either individually or in combination' and 'The best approach to sound sentencing is to leave it to the judiciary to exercise their experience and judgment' without any new device such as a Sentencing Council. The views of 'penologists, criminologists and bureaucrats in government departments . . . should not be allowed to prevail so as to impose a sentencing regime which is incomprehensible or unacceptable to right-thinking people generally' and the 1991 Act is implied to be a weak

---

[8] (1993) 14 Cr App R (S) 479.

[9] Taylor, Lord, 'Judges and sentencing', *Journal of the Law Society of Scotland*, April 1993.

measure 'more suited to gentler times'. After an offender has been given probation, conditional discharges and a community service order, Lord Taylor argued, 'there must surely be a custodial sanction available'. If people from the prison world were in the audience, they must have sighed when they heard Lord Taylor add that custody need not be 'a university of crime', since 'a more discriminating allocation of prisoners to suitable establishments with training facilities may well be capable of effecting reform and rehabilitation'. That was a classic example of the technique of sliding over prison problems by making unrealistic claims.

As for the 1991 Act, Lord Taylor said that its drafting had 'caused English criminal lawyers to tear their hair' but there were two specific problems. The first was the limitation of the seriousness test to two offences being sentenced at the same time, on which Lord Taylor repeated the example given by Lord Ackner during the Bill's passage of a person who stole £50 from his employer every week over a long period. The second problem was the treatment of previous convictions. On this Lord Taylor said that the Act required that two burglars charged with the same offence had to be treated in the same way notwithstanding that one was a first offender while the other had five previous convictions for burglary and had breached probation orders and failed to comply with community service orders. That interpretation of the Act is, of course, not in line with Lord Taylor's own judgment in *Bexley* and *Cox*, though it must have been music to the ears of all who believed in sentencing on record. In the event, the Gleneagles speech firmly planted the idea that the Act prohibited any account being taken of a defendant's criminal record, and within days the most extraordinary and fanciful assertions were being made. In an article in *The Times* on 25 March, for example, the Conservative ex-minister Alan Clark wrote that 'officials have deftly come up with an Act that makes it almost impossible for the bench, in over half the cases that come before it, to award a custodial sentence'. By that time Kenneth Clarke had made it known that he wanted to discuss the problems of the Act with the Lord Chief Justice and Lord Taylor's 'ill-fitting straitjacket' had joined unit fines as an object of constant ridicule in the press.

While all this had been going on, a highly technical Criminal Justice Bill on financial crime and jurisdictional extent had been going through Parliament. On 13 May Kenneth Clarke told the House of Commons that he had been advised that it would be possible to use it to amend the provisions of the 1991 Act that had given trouble, and that he proposed to do this so as to ensure that the law allowed the courts to exercise judgment and common sense. Specifically, the unit fine scheme would be abolished; section 1 of the 1991 Act would be amended to allow courts to take into account all the offences for which a defendant was being sentenced; and the power to have regard to the full criminal record of an offender and his response to previous sentences would be 'restored' to courts by repealing section 29. This sudden rejection of major components of an Act that had only been in force for seven months could have been embarrassing for Clarke but in the event he had a huge Parliamentary success. First, Tony Blair unaccountably decided to lead on the alleged bugging of the Royal Family's telephone conversations, and never really recovered his momentum. Then Robert Maclennan, speaking for the Liberal Democrats, exposed himself to a cutting riposte by excitedly accusing Clarke of 'effrontery and lack of sense'. Seizing the moment, Clarke asked him 'to go away, lie down in a dark room, keep taking the tablets, and think carefully about whether the Liberal Democrats have an opinion one way or the other on the merits of any of the proposals that I have just announced'.[10] This demonstration of genial brutality was received with acclamation and Clarke, who had told a Conservative audience the previous day that he was not as concerned as some about the size of the prison population,[11] left the chamber in triumph. The next day a leader in *The Times* praised him for 'having shown that a potential humiliation can be turned into a victory for common sense'. A fortnight later, on 18 May, Clarke was appointed Chancellor of the Exchequer and Michael Howard succeeded him as Home Secretary.

When the amendments that Clarke had announced were incorporated into the Criminal Justice Bill the simplest was the relaxation of the multiple offence provision that had limited courts to taking account of a maximum of two associated offences. The amendment to section 29, on previous convictions, was more problematic. During the Bill's committee stage the government accepted the Court of Appeal's repeated view that an offender should not be sentenced twice for the same offence.[12] The Labour opposition were not clear that the government's amendment achieved that, and put down an amendment at report stage, arguing that without a statement of proportionality on the face of the statute the law 'could return, not to the position before the 1991 Act . . . but a more punitive sentencing framework, under which some offenders could be given sentences out of all proportion to what they deserve'.[13] The Labour amendment was withdrawn, however, and the government amendment went ahead so that section 29 simply enabled a court considering the seriousness of an offence 'to take into account any previous convictions of the offender or any other failure of his to respond to previous sentences'. This is an ambivalent formula and we discuss it below. The unit fine amendments were the ones that were debated most thoroughly, as

---

[10] Hansard HC, 13 May 1993, col. 943.
[11] *The Guardian*, 13 May 1993.
[12] Hansard HC Standing Committee B, 17 June 1993, col. 289.
[13] Hansard HC, 29 June 1993, col. 906.

Labour wanted the government to retain the general principle of means-related fines but to give the courts more flexibility than they were allowed under the 1991 Act's highly prescriptive scheme. But the government were adamant on total abolition and the whole unit fine system was repealed and replaced by a simple provision requiring courts to take account of offenders' financial circumstances before fixing fines.

When the amended Bill went back to the House of Lords it gave an opportunity for Lord Ackner (by then retired) to recall the warnings he had given during the passage of the 1991 Act and to state the independence of the judiciary in the most extreme terms. In particular, he claimed that 'The government decided to ignore the doctrine of separation of powers'.[14] Later in his speech he explained that judicial independence meant that the judiciary should be able to do its job without interference from the *executive*, but he had come within a hair's breadth of claiming that it was in some way unconstitutional for the legislature to lay down any rules for the making of sentencing decisions within the statutory maxima. Such a claim is quite clearly constitutionally unsound, and it was to be explicitly surrendered in the next round of contention between the government and the judges, in 1997. Ackner's comment in 1993 can be seen as the high water mark of judicial triumphalism.

The *Cunningham* judgment and the statutory amendments decided by Kenneth Clarke had left the 1991 Act looking distinctly battered, but there was one major issue on which it was still open to the Court of Appeal to push forward the development of a principled body of law in the spirit of the 1990 White Paper. This was the 'custody threshold', the level of offence seriousness that divided imprisonment from community sentences. Without a much clearer delineation of this vital issue, which could only be done cumulatively by developing case law, much of the Act's structure fell away. It is not in practice possible, for example, to apply the *Queen* principle of a proportionality-based ceiling and progressive loss of mitigation unless the ceiling for the offence is generally recognisable. Sadly, the Court of Appeal has not taken a vigorous approach to this issue, and has accepted a variety of quite minor offending behaviour as meeting the criterion of seriousness for a custodial sentence. One of the most notorious cases was *Keogh*,[15] where the Court upheld a sentence of one month's imprisonment for obtaining £35-worth of goods by deception at a do-it-yourself store checkout. As Andrew Ashworth has commented,[16] a court that takes the view that such an offence is so serious that only custody can be justified 'is emptying the custody threshold of all meaning, and undermining any policy of restraint'.

---

[14] Hansard HL, 26 July 1993, col. 1090.
[15] (1994) 15 Cr App R (S) 279.
[16] In *Sentencing and Criminal Justice* (London: Butterworths, 1995), p. 238.

The situation contains a further ironic twist in that the 1991 Act repealed the special sentencing restrictions that had been created for young offenders in the 1980s, as described in chapter 7, and replaced them with its own simple (and seemingly ineffective) test of seriousness.

In a speech on 11 November 1993[17] Lord Taylor said that the philosophy of the 1991 Act still held good and that the amendments had improved it and made it more realistic. A dispassionate assessment from the vantage point of 1997, however, would come to a gloomy view about the achievement of most of the main objectives of the Act, other than the stabilisation of early release arrangements through the scheme proposed by the Carlisle committee. In the next four paragraphs we consider fines, previous convictions, and the impact on the prison population.

The proportionate use of fines for indictable offences in magistrates' courts has fallen from 45 per cent in 1991 to 36 per cent in 1996. The declining trend was briefly reversed in the last quarter of 1992, when the 1991 Act was brought into force, but the rate fell sharply throughout 1993 (i.e., preceding the repeal of unit fines by the 1993 Act). Figures collected by the Home Office showed that between the last quarters of 1992 and 1993 average fines rose by 18 per cent for unemployed people but decreased by 32 per cent for people in employment. Comparable figures are not available for later years, but it is unlikely that the inequality of impact of fines has since been reduced.

In his 11 November speech Lord Taylor specifically commented on the question of previous convictions by saying that the balance was now right between having regard to an offender's previous record and respecting the established rule that a person should not be punished twice for the same offence:

> The court will approach the question of seriousness, of course, by looking primarily at the instant offences which have to be dealt with, but looking at them not in a vacuum or in blinkers, but against a previous history.

Like the amended version of section 29 itself, Lord Taylor's formula was not entirely clear. The seriousness of an offence is a product of the harm that has been done and the culpability of the offender, and what Lord Taylor seems to have meant is that culpability may be increased by a previous bad record. What is at issue is the weight that should be given to each component, and the Court of Appeal has not yet given guidance on the way in which the 1993 amendment of section 29 should be interpreted.[18] Judging from political

---

[17] To the National Association for the Care and Resettlement of Offenders.

[18] Ashworth argues in *Sentencing and Criminal Justice*, p. 161, that a proper interpretation of the amended section 29 would have regard to ministers' comments during the passage of the 1993 Act, and would uphold the principle of proportionality and loss of mitigation, as pronounced in *Queen*.

comment, the general view seems to be that the 1993 amendment amounted to the re-establishment of a doctrine of aggravation for a bad record, so that repeat offenders guilty of quite petty offences can properly be sent to prison.

This is an important point of principle, and the argument about restrictions on taking account of previous convictions did a great deal to discredit the 1991 Act politically. How much difference it all made in practice in the courts is quite another matter, and the present authors are sceptical. There is every reason to believe that even before the 1991 Act the *Queen* doctrine was followed in the breach as much as in the observance. As for the Act's apparent restrictions, the basic fact is that the courts have applied the test of seriousness in such a very elastic way that no recognisable custody threshold has emerged for the less serious offences. In this absence of any sort of datum line it is hardly relevant whether one speaks in terms of a theoretical exercise of mitigation for a good record or of aggravation for a bad one. In the light of cases such as *Keogh* the sentencer who wants to send a petty repeat offender to prison can comfortably tell himself that even fairly trivial offences 'deserve' imprisonment and that it is only a clean record or some other compelling factor in mitigation that will shield the offender from custody.

It is painfully clear that the Act has not been successful in moderating the use of imprisonment through the 1990s, since all its relevant provisions remain in place and the courts are using imprisonment more freely than anyone can remember. Did it have any short-term effect? Some commentators have claimed that it began to work as intended, but was then effectively sabotaged by political means. The present authors doubt whether the evidence really bears that out. In October 1992, when the Act was brought into force, the imprisonment rate in the Crown Court dropped from 48 per cent to a historical low of 42 per cent, where it remained until January 1993. It then began to climb almost as quickly as it had fallen, so that by May 1993, when Kenneth Clarke announced his proposed amendments, it was up to 50 per cent (or 2 points higher than immediately before the Act took effect). The pattern in magistrates' courts was similar, with a drop from 5 to 2 per cent and then a climb back to 5 per cent again. Of course, these changes did not happen in a vacuum. As discussed at the beginning of this chapter, the first few months of 1993 were a period of increasingly punitive and condemnatory political rhetoric, and that has certainly been a major factor in sentencing during the subsequent years. Whether a change in the political climate could have produced such rapid and significant changes in sentencing as occurred in the first few months of 1993 is, in our view, much more doubtful. Whatever the full reasons for the drop in custodial sentencing at the moment the Act came into force, it seems to us that the courts very quickly reverted to their previous practice under their own initiative.

These assessments amount to a distinctly downbeat view of the practical impact of the 1991 Act, and in order to learn from the episode we need to ask what went wrong. It is fairly clear that one very major factor was the change in the make-up and political mood of the Conservative government between the conception of the Act's principles under Douglas Hurd and its unravelling under Kenneth Clarke. By that time two other Home Secretaries (David Waddington and Kenneth Baker) had come and gone, and no ministers at the Home Office had enough sense of ownership of the Act to want to take any risks in defending it. But, as we have seen, the things that tarnished the Act had all been predicted and did not suddenly emerge out of nowhere.

The scheme for administering unit fines was extremely rigid and was virtually guaranteed to give trouble when combined with an enormous increase in the level of fines. Some softer entry to the new regime, by capping fines in some way, might have reduced the problem. It was, in any event, a fairly heroic judgment that the Conservative Party would in general be happy to see middle-income offenders being fined, say, six times more severely for routine motoring offences, and it might have been worth remembering that such offences are excluded from the unit fines schemes that operate in Germany, a country that was often quoted as an excellent example to follow.

The debacle on previous convictions and on multiple offences was probably even more damaging, because it lay closer to the core of sentencing and the courts' ability to deal with serious offences. Whatever the courts' interpretation had been of the multiple offence provisions that operated for young offenders, there was surely no convincing answer to Lord Ackner's amendment to enable a series of similar offences to be taken into account, and opposing it was hardly calculated to win over the higher judiciary. As for the treatment of previous convictions, we have only been able to speculate about the reasons for the extraordinary drafting, but the fact remains that this was seen as one of the points of greatest interest right from the time of David Waddington's pre-publication press conference in 1990 to Lord Taylor's ominous press conference immediately before the Act came into force two years later. It still seems surprising that such a politically vivid — but essentially simple — topic could have gone through the whole Parliamentary process in such confusion.

At a deeper level, the Act's whole structure of making punishment subject to a graduated hierarchy of criteria based on no more than 'seriousness' of the offence proved to be totally inadequate. This takes us to the heart of the matter. Had ministers been secure that a genuine reforming partnership had been established with the senior judiciary, it might have made very good sense to establish such a sparse conceptual framework of basic principles within which detailed elaboration could grow. Without that partnership, the

Act's simple tests of seriousness were no more than thongs of gossamer that the judiciary observed with resentment and brushed aside with contempt. Unless the Court of Appeal was prepared to use the framework in a positive developmental way, it could hardly be expected that the insertion of a test of 'seriousness' would itself bring about a sea change among sentencers, since proportionality was already generally seen as the core of the existing tariff. If there had been any doubt that it was to be 'business as usual', it was removed by the *Cunningham* judgment that confirmed deterrence as a sentencing objective. From the judges' point of view, the idea of deterrence was so deep-rooted that it may have been genuinely inconceivable that the government could have intended to remove it simply by making no mention of it.

The 1991 Act did both too much and too little. It boldly entered the holy ground of sentencing practice, attracting the vehement repudiation of Lord Taylor's Gleneagles speech, but it was too vague to get the business done. If the government had really been determined to regulate sentencing and stabilise the prison population through this kind of structure, it would have been necessary to anchor it in the real world by specifying the custody threshold with concrete criteria related to particular kinds of offence. That might or might not have been an unrealistically difficult proposition, both politically and with the judges, but the alternative has turned out to have been so ineffective as to be unreal. We may never know quite why the government believed so confidently in 1990 that the judiciary would eagerly cooperate in developing the ideas of the White Paper, when there was so much evidence of their fierce possessiveness over the 'art' of sentencing.

The inherent difficulties were almost certainly increased by the technicalities of proceeding by way of conventional primary legislation. An Act of Parliament does not have to look like the 1991 Act. It is possible for legislation to be constructed much more imaginatively and much more flexibly. If, for example, the legislation had included a statement of principles that was subject to amendment by secondary legislation, it is just conceivable that it might have been more viable. The question of deterrence might have been much better dealt with by, for example, stating that seriousness was to be the main criterion, and that if sentencers thought that a deterrent element was also needed they should state their reasons. Be all that as it may, the conclusion that we draw is that it will be a long time before any government will want to follow the example of the 1991 Act and attempt to structure sentencing practice within a network of statutory criteria that it is necessarily for the judiciary themselves to interpret. When the time comes to revisit sentencing policy — and we hope it will be soon — we think that the approach should be to establish a much more general objective with the judiciary, on the basis of which they should construct arrangements about which they have a sense of ownership.

10   'Prison Works'

From the peak of over 51,000 in 1988 when Douglas Hurd had been forced to use Army camps as prisons, the prison population had declined to the very low figure of 40,600 at the end of 1992. That soundbite figure was especially low because it reflected both the normal seasonal trough and the ephemeral effects surrounding the introduction of the 1991 Act. Nevertheless, even when the population increased through 1993, as the courts raised their imprisonment rate, the population remained under the certified normal accommodation level for nearly all the year because the building programme was bringing significant numbers of new places into use. Overcrowding did continue at local prisons, but 1993 was nevertheless the one year during the last few decades when the prison system was not operating under conditions of general systemic overcrowding, and at the same time the programme of reform flowing from the Woolf report was visibly delivering real change. To many people working in the system it seemed the beginning of much better times. At the same time, the markedly more punitive tone of the popular press continued while the political parties prepared their positions for the autumn conferences. In the last week of September a MORI poll found that the Conservative lead on law and order was down to 2 per cent, from 14 per cent immediately before the 1992 general election.

On 30 September Tony Blair was warmly applauded at the Labour Party conference for a speech that was very different in tone from anything heard there before. Hooligans, muggers, perverted rapists and racist thugs should be kept out of society 'until they learn to behave like human beings'; while better measures needed to be developed to protect and help the victims of crime, and programmes of punishment and rehabilitation were needed within the community. Before closing with the traditional 'tough on crime' formula, Blair threw down the gauntlet by announcing that 'Labour is the party of law and order in Britain today'. *The Times* leader commented that 'Mr Blair with his promise to put the victim at the heart of the criminal justice system [has] parked his tanks on Michael Howard's lawn'.[1]

The Conservative Party conference was preceded by a flurry of speculation in the press about the Conservative Party's confidence in John Major's leadership, and the whole occasion was orchestrated to signal a change of direction to the right. Howard's speech on 6 October came after the appearance of a victim of a sexual attack, who spoke harrowingly about her ordeal, and after a warm-up by Lord Archer of Weston-super-Mare, who attacked, among other things, the 'trendy *Guardian* and *Observer* arts pages'. When Howard spoke, after almost five months as Home Secretary, he set out an agenda of 27 heavily slanted law and order proposals, and broke with the policy of a century by declaring that 'Prison works'. The proposals were a mixed bag, including more demanding community service orders, restrictions on bail and on cautioning, limitation of the 'right to silence' of accused persons, and new laws against squatters. Howard went out of his way to mark out new political territory when he said, 'This may mean that more people will go to prison. I do not flinch from that. We shall no longer judge the success of our system of justice by a fall in the prison population.' To make it clear that the new policy of more imprisonment was for real, Howard announced a programme of six new prisons, to be provided by the private sector under the powers that had been taken in the 1991 Act. On the next day, 7 October, John Major unveiled to the conference his campaign that 'It is time to get back to basics, to self-discipline and respect for the law', and undertook that the legislation to implement many of Howard's 27 points would be the centrepiece of the next year's legislative programme. Major set out his view on crime, to the effect that understanding and persuasion had been tried and failed, and that a harsher approach was necessary.

We do not know in how much detail this change of policy had been planned at the time of Major's announcement of a 'crusade against crime' the previous February, but everything that had unfolded in the government's response to crime since that time had certainly been in a consistent direction, including Kenneth Clarke's statement of 20 February, which concluded that he was less concerned about the prison population than some people, and that it should be 'driven by the decision of the courts'. Be that as it may, Howard's 'Prison works' speech marks the generally recognised start of an open race between the two major parties on law and order, with the Conservative government producing ever more extreme proposals and the

---

[1] *The Times*, 2 October 1993.

Labour party being sometimes equivocal, sometimes even harsher than the government, but never allowing itself to be trapped in a position of outright opposition such as might expose it, however unreasonably, to the gibe of being soft on crime.

There was nothing in Howard's 'Prison works' speech that directly affected the position of the judges, though some proposals in it, such as the limitation of the 'right of silence', obviously raised issues on which the judges could be expected to express an opinion. In so far as the government's message was that it was for the courts alone to settle the size of the prison population through their decisions in individual cases, that was exactly what judges themselves had always been saying. Nevertheless, a number of judges were left feeling uncomfortable by the speech's general encouragement of high sentencing and its assertions that imprisonment 'worked' in a way to which they did not subscribe.

In the event, the first senior judge to make an implied criticism of the new direction of government policy was Lord Woolf, who approached the question from the position of a prison reformer who saw the improvements in prison conditions with which his name was associated being threatened by the prospect of unregulated overcrowding. In a wide-ranging, speculative and notably liberal speech to the New Assembly of Churches on 12 October he warned against overcrowding being the most corrosive influence on the prison system, threatening instability and rioting and imperilling the maintenance of rehabilitative programmes. He also canvassed a variety of suggestions for much wider social reform, such as the possibility of legalising some drugs and penalising people who did not adequately protect their own property. Most significantly, he entered the political arena by saying, 'Statements are being made that having tried the soft option and that having failed, now is the time to get tough on crime. Such talk is short-sighted and irresponsible.' This was followed by an article in the *Observer* on 17 October in which Lord Ackner and five serving judges summarised their views on imprisonment. These were by no means outlandishly ultra-liberal, and the judges expressed them in a reasonable and non-confrontational way, though two of the judges expressed sympathy with some of Woolf's ideas and Lord Ackner did say that both political parties had a paranoiac attitude towards being thought soft on crime. What really emerged, however, were the usual mainstream concerns about the damaging effects of prison, the need to use it as a punishment of last resort, and a general attitude that was not easily compatible with an attitude of 'Prison works'.

All this was played back to ministers by the press, which led to Major and Howard both confirming that 'Prison does work'. In the House of Commons Major expressed his belief that prison was effective as a punishment as well as a deterrent,[2] while Howard spelt out that 'Thousands of dangerous criminals are prevented from attacking the community while they are inside. And many who might commit crimes are deterred from doing so.'[3] Questioned on 'The World This Weekend' about the judges' views in the *Observer* article, Howard stood firm on the proposition that his aim was to achieve a criminal justice system that protected the public, and that he would not be deflected from that target.

At the end of this lively fortnight Lord Taylor appeared on the 'Question Time' television programme on 28 October and evidently tried to pour oil on the troubled waters by saying that he agreed in general with the contents of Howard's conference speech, while adding that he was 'not sure he approved of the tone of it all'. He also said, significantly, that 'I don't think we should send people to prison for longer and longer sentences. Villains don't ask if they are going to get three or five years. They ask whether they are going to get caught.' We are sure that this trenchant comment hits the nail smack on the head, but if it was so clear in 1993 that a stiff dose of scepticism is in order when considering the alleged deterrent effects of sentence lengths, it is hard to see why the Court of Appeal found it necessary to go so far out of its way to retain deterrence as an aim of sentencing in the *Cunningham* judgment less than a year previously.

Looking back, it is now clear that what happened in 1993 was a symmetrical reversal of roles between the government and the judiciary, with the cusp marked by Lord Ackner's assertion of judicial supremacy in July 1993. The judiciary began the year by reacting against a principled (albeit faulty) piece of legislation that sought to impose some structure on their sentencing decisions and which they may well have seen as impliedly casting them in the role of punitive problem-makers who were inflating the prison population by sentencing more than was warranted by the seriousness of offences. After Howard's 'Prison works' speech they were reacting to a populist policy that appeared to encourage more imprisonment by whatever argument came to hand. It looks as though some of the senior judges immediately realised that Howard's policy was inherently likely to develop in a way that cast them in the role of indulgent liberals whose weak sentencing was failing to protect potential victims.

'Prison works' is, of course, a perfectly crafted example of a political slogan that is so adroitly sited on the borderline between the meaningful, the meaningless and the implied that it is virtually proof against rational interrogation. In fact, nobody would question Howard's statements that people in prison cannot attack the public and that the existence of the penal system is a deterrent. Simply stating such propositions, however, implies the

---

[2] Hansard HC, 19 October 1993, col. 144.
[3] *The Times*, 15 October 1993.

existence of opponents who refuse to accept them. Similarly, the single-issue line that public protection is the paramount aim of the criminal justice system carries the implication that anyone who questions proposals that are put forward under that banner must lack concern for the public. Devices of this kind are extremely difficult to handle politically. They have been instrumental in reshaping penal policy in the USA, and they appear to be doing just the same in this country.

Initially, the government went out of its way to position the Criminal Justice and Public Order Bill, implementing many of Howard's 27 points, as the centrepiece of its 'back to basics' campaign, and this was the line taken by Howard himself on 10 November 1993 when he gave the clearest possible encapsulation of the Conservative position on personal responsibility. What he said was, 'We should have no truck with trendy theories that try to explain away crime by blaming socio-economic factors. Criminals . . . should be held to account for their actions and punished accordingly. Trying to pass the buck is wrong, counter-productive and dangerous.'[4] Already by 11 January 1994, however, when the Bill had its second reading in the Commons, the 'back to basics' campaign had largely unravelled because it had been sold as an attempt to roll back the permissive society and was thus discredited by a rash of scandals involving Conservative politicians. Leading for the Opposition, Tony Blair scoffed at Howard's claim on the radio that the government had been hamstrung in their fight against crime because their civil servants had forced them to accept the nostrums of the liberal establishment. He went on to give what still remains one of the firmest statements of the Labour Party's policy towards prison expansion and dealing with the causes of crime, saying:

We face a choice. We can either go in the direction of the United States where there are 1.25 million people in gaol . . . and violent crime has continued to rise. Alternatively, we can understand that it is important to combine programmes of reform and prevention with the strengthening of the criminal justice system. The Home Secretary's policy of 'Prison works' will not succeed.[5]

This debate was the first occasion when the Labour Party adopted what became their normal tactics of abstaining on Howard's law and order legislation.

The Criminal Justice and Public Order Act 1994 did contain some provisions that directly affected prisons. These included powers for private businesses to design, construct, maintain and finance new prisons (including

[4] *The Times*, 11 November 1993.
[5] Hansard HC, 11 January 1994, cols 37–8.

the six that Howard had announced in the 'Prison works' speech), and a provision prohibiting anyone from inducing prison officers to withhold their services. For the purpose of this account, however, we need not look in detail at any more of the Conservative government's law and order legislation until the Crime (Sentences) Bill which was unveiled at the Conservative Party conference in 1995.

Before leaving the Criminal Justice and Public Order Bill, though, we need to note the puzzling affair of the 193 burglars, which was destined to run on to the last weeks of the Conservative government. We have already commented that the 'Prison works' policy was impliedly justified by a range of arguments including retribution, deterrence and incapacitation. Although deterrence and retribution would continue to figure in the Conservative government's rationales, it was incapacitation that steadily moved forward to become the main justification. Among the arguments that Home Office ministers used to support the argument that 'Prison works' was a piece of research on a sample of 193 people who were convicted of residential burglary and given community service orders in 1987. This study was used to support the proposition that between 3 and 13 burglaries would be prevented for each convicted burglar imprisoned for a year, but on the day before the Bill's second reading Tony Blair released a commentary by Home Office statisticians. This concluded that the comparison was problematical for several reasons, including the small size of the sample and the fact that some of the convictions recorded against the people given community service orders would have been for offences committed previously. The latter point was a familiar technical problem in making comparisons of this kind.[6] A Home Office spokesman said that, while there were problems in comparing prison and community punishments, ministers stood by their claim that prison worked in preventing burglaries while criminals were behind bars.[7] The reason why we mention this incident now is that the same rather trifling sample would be used to illustrate the incapacitatory effect of imprisonment in the White Paper proposing mandatory sentences two years later, when it unsurprisingly precipitated much argument.

By June 1994 public opinion polls were finding that Labour had established a lead over the Conservatives on law and order[8] and the government soon lifted the profile of the 'Prison works' project. Although, as we have said, it was unprecedented in the 20th century for the government to give general encouragement for more imprisonment, the project that Howard had

---

[6] As described at the end of this chapter, the same technical point about measuring the reconvictions of people given community service orders was to feature in an argument about ministerial comments on some of the very last figures released by the Home Office before the general election.

[7] *The Guardian*, 11 January 1994.

[8] *The Times*, 1 June 1994.

unveiled did not go so far as openly to criticise the courts for being too lenient. John Major crossed that line in a heavily publicised speech to the Social Market Foundation on 9 September 1994, when he is reported as demanding an unambiguous message from the courts and calling for tougher sentences for all crime, both petty and serious. Catching a criminal was of little use, he said, unless he received a sentence that 'straightens him out and deters others'.[9] There had seldom been a penal policy quite like this, let alone from the Prime Minister of the day, and Major stamped his message with the classic Conservative line on personal responsibility by saying, 'Too often we have excused crime, patronising people as if nothing better could be expected of them'. *The Times* leader the next day commented that little had enraged Tory party strategists more than that Labour had overtaken them as the party of law and order, while *The Guardian* noted that opinion polls gave Labour a lead of more than 34 per cent and commented that Major's hold on power was 'contingent'.

The constantly steepening trajectory of the Conservative government's imprisonment policy from the time of Major's 'crusade against crime' in February 1993 continued with Howard following Major's overt criticism of the courts in a speech to the Police Superintendents' Association on 3 October 1995 when he spoke of there being 'still public dismay over sentencing'[10] and expressed surprise at the rate at which burglars were sent to prison and at the sentences they received. That tone of overt criticism of the courts was spectacularly developed a few days later at the Conservative Party conference when the party chairman, Dr Brian Mawhinney, told the conference on 10 October that judges and magistrates did not act in a vacuum, 'so praise them when you agree with them and let them know when you are dissatisfied, always remembering that of course they have heard all the evidence. The expression of the public's view on sentencing does have an effect.'[11] Since the public (apart from those who are directly involved in cases) can only get to know of sentences via the media's account of them, and since much of the popular press was committed to a simple law and order agenda, the recruitment of direct public participation in the debate could only go in one direction. We are not going to be rash enough to assert that the increase in the imprisonment rate at this time was a direct matter of cause and effect, but it is a fact that the imprisonment rate in the Crown Court, which had been rising throughout 1995, climbed steeply in the closing months of the year.

The proposals that Howard made at the conference were for two sets of changes that were manifestly modelled very closely on what was happening

---

[9] *The Times*, 10 September 1994.
[10] *The Times*, 4 October 1995.
[11] *The Times*, 11 October 1995.

in the USA. First, Howard claimed that the existing (i.e., Carlisle committee) system of sentencing made a mockery of the courts, with prisoners serving only half or two thirds of their sentences in prison. It was therefore 'time to get honesty back into sentencing'; prisoners should only be able to get a small amount off their sentences, and should have to earn that by model ~~Priues~~ behaviour. Second, there was 'a strong case for greater certainty in sentencing — for stiff minimum sentences for burglars and dealers in hard drugs who offend again and again and again' and also 'a strong case for saying that anyone convicted for the second time of a serious violent or sexual offence should receive an automatic sentence of life imprisonment'. Each part of the policy came with its slogan. The honesty in sentencing provisions were characterised as representing 'no more half-time sentences for full-time crimes', whilst mandatory minimum sentences articulated the proposition that 'If you don't want to do the time, don't do the crime'. Howard said that he wanted to know what the judges thought of his proposals.

The simultaneous espousal of both of the most controversial aspects of current American sentencing practices was generally attributed in the press to Howard's hope that he would eventually find ground onto which the Labour Party would not follow him. There was an additional reason for the adoption of the 'honesty in sentencing' proposals, however. The Learmont report on prison security was due to be published only four days after Howard's speech. Learmont's undistinguished report took a simple view of early release systems and completely disregarded the Carlisle committee's analysis of the history of the matter. For Learmont it was a simple question of incentives and he had no problem in declaring that 'if every day by which release was brought forward had to be earned . . . a cornerstone of good behaviour throughout the period of sentence would be laid'. No Home Secretary would be in a rush to reject the advice that was publicly offered him on security in the politically embarrassing aftermath of the Whitemoor and Parkhurst escapes, and if earned early release was to be on the agenda ~~Policy~~ there were obvious political attractions for Howard in expanding the idea to constitute an 'honesty of sentencing' regime with the amount of early release severely limited.

Immediately after Howard's conference speech, Lord Taylor issued a press notice declaring that mandatory sentences were inconsistent with doing justice, adding that:

> Long sentences, sometimes very long sentences, are necessary in some cases to protect the public. But I do not believe that the threat of longer and longer periods of imprisonment across the board will deter habitual criminals. What deters them is the likelihood of being caught, which at the moment is small.

Howard's urbane reply was, 'He is entitled to his opinion. Most police officers take a different view.'[12] It was as unprecedented for a Home Secretary to identify himself with the police in opposing the views of a Lord Chief Justice as it had been for Lord Taylor to issue his press notice in the first place. Howard had given Taylor three days' notice of the contents of his conference speech,[13] and Taylor, who had been pleading in the press for better understanding of the judiciary's task, may have been provoked beyond human endurance by Mawhinney's fomentation of popular complaint against the judges in the meantime. Be that as it may, the dispute between the Conservative government and the judiciary had taken a further ugly step.

The next developments came in March 1996 when Lord Taylor gave an important lecture at King's College, London, the government published a White Paper setting out their proposals for legislation, and Jack Straw (who had succeeded Tony Blair as the Labour Party's shadow Home Secretary in 1994) issued a paper that laid out Labour Party policy on sentencing.

In his lecture[14] Lord Taylor said that he had intended to wait for the White Paper before commenting further, but believed it was now his duty to clarify the motivation of the judiciary's objections, since these were being misrepresented. He accepted without question Parliament's constitutional right to legislate for minimum mandatory sentences and denied that the judges' objections were due to a jealous protection of judicial independence. Neither would it be right for him, as an independent judge, to express any view on the consequences of the government's proposals on the prison population. The fundamental objection to minimum sentences was simply that they would cause injustice by fettering the judge's discretion to take account of all the circumstances of the offence and the offender. Further objections were the possible effect of discouraging guilty pleas and, in the case of a rapist facing a mandatory life sentence, the possible encouragement to kill his victim since the penalty for murder would be no greater. Last, it was likelihood of detection that primarily deterred crime, not a harsher and more rigid sentencing regime. 'All the wishful thinking in the world will not convince anyone that crime in America has fallen because of their sentencing policy.' On one issue, however, Lord Taylor found that he could agree with Howard's ideas. Provided that sentences were adjusted so that prisoners did not serve longer, there was merit in the proposal to bring sentences actually to be served closer to the nominal sentences pronounced in court. Using a phrase on which the government would later seize, Lord Taylor described the sentencing exercise in court as having 'the appearance of a charade'. When

---

[12] *The Times*, 13 October 1995.

[13] Rozenberg, J., *Trial of Strength* (London: Richard Cohen Books, 1997), p. 53.

[14] Taylor, Lord, 'Continuity and change in the criminal law', King's College, London, 6 March 1996.

the White Paper[15] was published it did very little to assuage the kind of doubts that Lord Taylor had expressed. On 'honesty in sentencing' the proposal was that early release should be limited to 20 per cent of the sentence, or in practice rather less. With an approving reference to Learmont, it was proposed that for the first 12 months prisoners should be able to earn up to six days a month by cooperation, while above 12 months there would be three days a month to be earned by cooperation and a further three days by positive good behaviour, hard work and compliance. Supervision after release from a sentence of 12 months or more would be for three months or 15 per cent of the sentence, whichever was longer. Judges would be expected to take account of the new release arrangements when passing sentence, so there should be no general increase in the prison population.

The White Paper's proposals for mandatory sentences for violent or sexual offenders, drug traffickers and burglars were each to be made subject to a let-out provision for 'genuinely exceptional circumstances'. Offenders who were convicted twice of an offence that came from a specified list of violent or sexual offences that already carried a maximum sentence of life imprisonment would get life on the second conviction. Offenders who were convicted of three offences of trafficking in class A drugs would get seven years on the third conviction. Three-time domestic burglars would get three years on the third conviction but, unlike the other two categories, it would only be convictions after the commencement of the Act that would count. Statistics were given to illustrate the practice of the courts in the various categories that the proposals would affect. In particular, it was noted that in 1994 there had been 217 people who were convicted of a second violent or sexual offence that carried a maximum sentence of life imprisonment, but that only 10 of them had actually been given life. As for burglars, details were given of a 1993–4 sample of 949 in the Crown Court and 1,215 in the magistrates' courts. These showed that average sentences in the Crown Court rose from 16.2 months on a first burglary conviction to 18.9 months on a third, with the corresponding figures for magistrates' courts being 3.7 and 4.0 months. On third convictions the Crown Court was imprisoning 75 per cent and the magistrates 36 per cent.

Finally, the White Paper made estimates of the cost of all these proposals, which it acknowledged would lead to a substantial increase in the prison population over time. It made the assumption that the deterrent effect of the mandatory sentencing regime would reduce the requirement for prison places by 20 per cent. It also assumed that the regime would not have any significant effect on the sentences for other offenders (so that the mandatory three years for a third-time domestic burglar would not have any impact on

---

[15] *Protecting the Public* (Cm 3190) (London: HMSO, 1996).

the sentencing of second-time domestic burglars or on burglars of commercial premises). On those assumptions (plus the belief that judges would reduce their sentences to compensate for the 'honesty in sentencing' scheme) the mandatory life and seven-year sentences for violent and drug offenders could be brought into force in October 1997, while the rest should wait until October 1999 since the minimum sentence for burglars would 'need to be implemented once a prison building programme was under way to provide the necessary places'. Twelve additional privately financed prisons could come on stream at the rate of one or two a year from 2001/02. Together with some rebuilding and houseblocks on the existing estate, this would provide 12,600 places by 2011/12, when the proposals would have led to 10,800 extra prisoners. By the same time the extra cost of the project would be between £375 million and £435 million a year.

Jack Straw's paper, *Honesty, Consistency and Progression in Sentencing*, had also come out in March. This paper, for the Home Affairs Committee of the Parliamentary Labour party, is important, since it is quite a detailed statement of the agenda to which the Labour government remains broadly committed. The paper covers a lot of ground (such as the falling proportion of offences that result in a conviction and the organisation of the Crown Prosecution Service) that goes well beyond our subject. We shall simply summarise what it said on the three key points listed in its title. *Honesty* is the most straightforward of these. On this, the paper proposed that, in so far as there was a problem with the sentence to be served being different from the nominal sentence, it could be completely and cleanly met by the court pronouncing the full effect of the sentence at the time it was passed.

Consistency and *progression* are much deeper issues. Straw's paper begins by noting that 'Prison cannot fail to work to stop offending outside while an offender is inside. That — i.e., public safety — and punishment, must be among the principal purposes of custody. It is, however, a foolish society which does not demand of the huge investment we all make in the cost of the prison service that it better reforms those in its charge.' The paper then goes on to look at the sentencing practice of the courts. It shows the discrepancies in the use of custody between different Crown Courts (where the custody rate varied between 38 and 67 per cent) and between magistrates' courts (where the highest custody rate for indictable offences was 10 times the lowest). On *progression* the paper quotes figures for a three-week sample that Straw had obtained from the Home Office, showing that there was little progression in the severity of sentencing for repeated drug and burglary offending. The paper concludes that the sentencing system:

must be more consistent than it has been, and that there is more progression in sentencing. In every other situation — at home, at school, in the workplace — account is always taken of what amounts to previous offending behaviour. Indeed, this is built in to most workplace disciplinary procedures, and reflected in employment law. So it should within the court system.

As for the delivery system for achieving these changes, the paper rehearses the Labour Party's previous support for a Sentencing Council, and notes that 'we may end up with a formal Sentencing Council'. Before getting to that, however, Straw argues that we should look at how the existing system can be made to work better and more accountably, and the paper proposes that the Court of Appeal 'should be given a formal, proactive role to consult on and then deliver a system of sentencing guidelines for all offences'. In particular 'such guidelines should give particular attention to the sentencing of repeat offenders to ensure that proper account is taken of progression in sentencing'.

Straw's paper is completely silent on the resource costs of the progressive (i.e., cumulative) sentencing regime that it advocates. Its only reference to costs is a short comment on Howard's proposals for mandatory minimum sentences. The paper says — reasonably enough — that 'the public and Parliament will need to be satisfied as to what these proposals are likely to cost, what the benefits may be — and from where the money is to come'. For some reason, the Labour Party showed itself to be very easily satisfied on the matter and, in the event, Howard's proposals went through Parliament without any significant scrutiny whatsoever of the resource implications.

On 23 May 1996 Lord Taylor initiated a debate on the White Paper in the House of Lords while he was still Lord Chief Justice.[16] Taylor, who was exceptionally respected for his openness and personal qualities, was mortally ill and his impending retirement and replacement by Sir Thomas Bingham (now Lord Bingham of Cornhill) had already been announced. He began by saying, 'I venture to suggest that never in the history of our criminal law have such far-reaching proposals been put forward on the strength of such flimsy and dubious evidence' and went on to explain that his previously indicated support for the principle of 'honesty in sentencing' had been conditional on the management of the question being given careful thought, which had not happened. To expect the Lord Chief Justice to preside over the general reduction of sentencing levels when ministers were urging tougher sentences unamended, on the grounds that Labour had not opposed the provisions in the Commons, would cast the judiciary in the role of apparently thwarting the will of Parliament. Minimum sentences, he said, must involve a denial of justice. The White Paper's importation of 'genuinely

---

[16] Hansard HL, 23 May 1996, col. 1025.

exceptional circumstances' would be no help. If the phrase was construed narrowly it would be a dead letter; if it was construed widely the judges would be accused of driving a coach and horses through the Act. For the former Master of the Rolls, Lord Donaldson of Lymington, the White Paper simply gave 'a message loud and clear . . . that the judges are not to be trusted'.[17]

The stage was now set for the government to introduce its legislation in the last session of Parliament before the general election. The Crime (Sentences) Bill, which had its second reading in the Commons on 4 November 1996, was closely in line with the White Paper, except that it contained provisions seeking to ensure that judges reduced their sentences so as to compensate for the shorter amount of early release that would be available under the 'honesty in sentencing' regime, and setting out a formula that judges should use to achieve that result. The White Paper's 'genuinely exceptional circumstances' that relieved a court from the duty of passing a mandatory sentence now appeared simply as 'exceptional circumstances' and in an interview published in *The Times* on 5 November the Lord Chancellor, Lord Mackay of Clashfern, confirmed that he had ensured the inclusion of the phrase to enable judges 'to deal justly with particular cases'.

The Labour Party had made it clear in advance that they would not be opposing the second reading of the Bill in the House of Commons, so that debate, on 4 November 1996, had a somewhat unreal quality. Everyone knew that if the Bill were to be changed at all, it would have to be done in the House of Lords.

Howard described the Bill as being 'designed to improve the protection of the public against serious, dangerous and persistent offenders, and to increase public confidence in the sentencing process', and he claimed that it would 'introduce the biggest step change in our criminal justice system this century'. He made four references to the Bill being supported by the police, including the statement that 'the President of the Police Superintendents' Association said that it was "in the national interest" that the proposals became law as quickly as possible, yet the Opposition have steadfastly refused to support them'. His basic proposition was that 'those who persistently offend should know with certainty that they will face a stiff penalty if they offend again', and he described Straw's counter-proposals as not being worthy of the name of a crime Bill.

During his speech Howard had been asked some awkward questions about the way in which the Bill required judges to calculate the sentences they should give under the Bill's scheme, and the periods of supervision that would then apply, and this topic was an uncovenanted gift to Straw when he

---

[17] Ibid., col. 1049.

replied. Although the Bill included provision for extended post-release supervision of sex offenders, other types of offender serving determinate sentences were bound to be supervised or at risk of being recalled to prison less under the Bill than they would be under the present law. This was because the Carlisle committee had done its job only too well in making every part of the sentence count. To make matters worse from the government's point of view, the proposed abolition of parole would mean that prisoners would be released from determinate sentences without any risk assessment, and the Bill as introduced included an elementary mistake in the provisions on the calculation of new-style sentences.

Straw found it easy to make some telling points out of this muddle, and he made it clear that Labour's method of achieving clarity in sentencing was the simple proposition that the judge should tell the truth about each sentence as it was passed. His general approach to the Bill, however, was fiercely to attack the government for the fact that recorded crime had doubled in their time in office while the number of convictions had fallen, and to argue that 'the need for consistency and progression applies to all offences and at every point in the offender's criminal career'.[18] As for the mandatory sentences, there was no issue between Labour and the government about securing tough sentences for repeat burglars and drug dealers[19] and Labour was in favour of the proposed automatic life sentences for repeat violent offenders, while having some doubt about the width of the qualifying offences and especially the inclusion of wounding with intent as one of them.[20] Before ending by claiming that the Bill did nothing to tackle the real problem of the gap between crime and convictions and the need for reform of the CPS and the youth justice system, Straw ridiculed Howard for having resiled from the rigid mandatory sentences he had promised the Conservative Party conference. According to him, the inclusion of the phrase 'exceptional circumstances' would give the courts a wide discretion.[21]

The rest of the debate was notable for speeches by three former Conservative Home Office ministers. Douglas Hurd and Kenneth Baker both put a good deal of distance between themselves and the Bill, while Sir Peter Lloyd, who had been Minister of State with responsibility for prisons, set out a comprehensive critique of the whole project. Hurd expressed Olympian disdain for Straw's politicking and went on to stress that public protection rested not just on locking offenders up for longer but on how prisoners behaved when they were released. That in turn depended on training, probation, work and education in prison, and if these things collapsed under

---

[18] Hansard HC, 4 November 1996, col. 926.
[19] Ibid., col. 927.
[20] Ibid., col. 930.
[21] Ibid., col. 931.

financial pressure 'We could add to the dangers facing the public while we claim to reduce them'.[22] Baker struck a similar tone, saying that the prisons were 'full not of professional criminals but of professional prisoners who go back again, again and again. . . . One way in which to help such people is to give them the skills to allow them to acquire even the humblest job.'[23] Lloyd argued that long sentences were not an effective deterrent, that reported crime had begun to fall before the prison population had started its rise, that the judges would be bound to overcompensate for the 'honesty in sentencing' regime, that the inevitable great rise in the prison population would pre-empt resources that could be better spent in fighting crime, that it was perverse to abolish parole since it was an effective system of public protection, and that the narrow discretion allowed by the phrase 'exceptional circumstances' would be bound to cause injustice and hard cases that would discredit the enterprise. Several Conservative backbenchers spoke in support of the Bill. The Liberal Democrat spokesman Alex Carlile launched a total attack, put down a reasoned amendment and divided the House against the Bill's second reading, but the government won a huge majority as the Labour Party abstained.

Nothing of much moment happened to the Bill in standing committee. When it went back to the full House of Commons for its remaining stages there were some thoughtful debates on, for example, psychiatric assessment and drug treatment programmes, but there were only two episodes that are relevant to the main story. On 13 January 1997 Straw unsuccessfully moved an amendment to place a duty on the Court of Appeal to consider and review sentencing practice and policy and from time to time to issue guidelines.[24] This 'delivery system', trailed in Straw's March 1996 paper, had now formally become the Labour Party's policy, replacing the idea of a Sentencing Council. Straw particularly emphasised the lack of progression shown by the figures quoted in his paper and said that 'The idea of proper progression, which I believe is accepted across the House, is not consistently translated into sentencing'.[25] When questioned by Howard about the effect of the Bill's mandatory sentences, he said, 'The vast range of offences and offenders will be unaffected. Therefore, the need for better machinery to secure consistency and progression will remain.'[26]

On 15 January 1997 the House of Commons had its last crack at the question of judicial discretion when a group of amendments was discussed that all had the purpose of allowing a court not to pass one of the mandatory

---

[22] Ibid., col. 936.
[23] Ibid., col. 943.
[24] Hansard HC, 13 January 1997, col. 74.
[25] Ibid., col. 77.
[26] Ibid., col. 78.

sentences if it was not in the interests of justice to do so. Labour were only concerned about wounding with intent being an offence that triggered the automatic life sentence. Lloyd was not concerned about the automatic life sentence, since the tariff would stay in the discretion of the judge, but he spoke powerfully about the injustices that would result from the mandatory sentences for drug offenders and burglars and repeatedly taunted the opposition for not joining in that substantive debate. Elfyn Llwyd, a Plaid Cymru member who had represented the minority parties in the committee stage, wanted to apply the interests of justice provision to all the mandatory penalties. He was joined in that by Alan Beith for the Liberal Democrats who also spoke about the long time-scale for the implementation of the government's proposals and the fact that the cost of the necessary extra prisons was not in its expenditure plans. Beith tartly exposed the cruel charade by saying, 'I believe that the Bill's provisions have a more political than penal purpose, and that the government do not seriously intend them to be carried out'.[27]

A very great deal of time had by now been wasted at all stages of the Bill on inconclusive debate about the meaning of 'exceptional circumstances' and how much discretion that would leave the courts. Given the courts' well-documented interpretation of the phrase in the context of other criminal statutes — and especially in the 1991 Act's provision to limit the use of suspended sentences — there could never have been the slightest real cause to doubt that they would continue to give it a narrow interpretation and would not regard as exceptional a wide range of circumstances that normally justified mitigation. Common examples would be the age of the offender, a long period free of offending or the small value of stolen property. The matter had, in fact, been made quite clear on 10 November 1996 by the Lord Chief Justice, Lord Bingham of Cornhill, who had explained on the BBC programme 'Breakfast with Frost' that 'exceptional' must mean 'very unusual' at the very least, and that most of the circumstances that had been mentioned in debate were not unusual. Lord Bingham had also said that 'It would mitigate the difficulty if the Bill provided that a judge should not be obliged to pass a mandatory sentence if he considered it, in all the circumstances, unjust to do so', since that would at least enable the judge to avoid passing a sentence that he believed to be 'simply anomalous'. David Maclean, the Home Office Minister of State, quoted this comment in making it clear that it was precisely for that reason that the government was opposed to any reference to justice. 'That would', said Maclean before the government won the vote on the amendments, 'make a nonsense of the concept and purpose of mandatory penalties and it would drive a coach and horses through the Bill'.[28]

---

[27] Hansard HC, 15 January 1997, col. 383.
[28] Ibid., col. 397.

Before the Bill was given its third reading and left the Commons the same day Straw said that the Opposition supported the principle of indeterminate life sentences for repeat rapists and others, while being concerned about wounding with intent as a qualifying offence. As for the mandatory determinate sentences, Straw simply prevaricated behind the proposition that ministers should have been much more explicit about what they meant by 'exceptional circumstances'. He worked in a passing reference to Howard's 'wildly optimistic assumptions about public spending'.[29]

Two things were obvious after the Bill left the Commons. First, there would clearly be some kind of confrontation between the government and the judges in the House of Lords on the question of qualifying the mandatory sentences by a reference to the interests of justice. The nature of the argument was encapsulated by Maclean's calculated rejection of the Lord Chief Justice's concern that judges would be forced to pass sentences that they believed to be anomalous. Second, the government's proposals on 'honesty in sentencing', and the abolition of the parole scheme, were patently ill prepared and extremely vulnerable to accusations of giving the public less protection than the current arrangements.

In the Lords' second reading debate on 27 January the Home Office Minister of State, Lady Blatch, pointedly referred to the Bill being supported by the elected chamber and expressed the hope that it would not be the subject of 'misplaced concern about the proper relationship between Parliament and the judiciary'.[30] The Labour spokesman Lord McIntosh of Haringey made it clear that his party intended to examine and probe the Bill very thoroughly, including the question of inserting an interests of justice test for the mandatory sentences and also including an examination of the effects on the prison population and on public expenditure (which never happened, in the event, in either House of Parliament). He was followed by the Liberal Democrat spokesman, Lord Rodgers of Quarry Bank, who was disappointed by the Labour Party's neutrality and trenchantly continued his party's attack on the whole project, which he saw as a 'bad Bill with few redeeming features'.[31]

Given the nature of the government's proposals, the sequence of events that had led up to them, and the open warfare between his predecessor and the government, Lord Bingham needed to make an exceptional speech if he was to articulate the depth of the judges' feelings without counter-productively raising the temperature. In the event, his speech[32] was a memorable occasion of Parliamentary oratory and forensic power. He took the studiously

---

[29] Ibid., col. 426.
[30] Hansard HL, 17 January 1997, col. 971.
[31] Ibid., col. 980.
[32] Ibid., col. 983–90.

moderate position of testing each of the Bill's main proposals by asking four questions. Will it be just? Will it serve to reduce levels of crime or increase the protection of society? Will it be cost-effective? Will it work in practice? While Bingham was eloquent on the injustice and practical evils flowing from mandatory sentencing, he did not restrict himself to the question of judicial discretion. By the time he came to his peroration, each main component of the Bill had been dissected and found to be misconceived. Against the clinical precision of his analysis it was all the more telling when Bingham closed by asking his hearers to remember that the people who would be affected by the Bill would predominantly be young men, who had in many cases experienced deprivation and various kinds of hardship. Bingham disowned any suggestion that they were innocent victims of determinist causes but suggested 'that in discharge of our duty to our fellow men we should, instead of spending billions on new prisons, double and redouble existing efforts to identify and treat delinquents . . . long before they are sucked into the destructive maw of the penal system'. Finally, Bingham referred to the wise, humane and moral thinking expressed in Churchill's famous prison reform speech of 1910 and contrasted it to the present day. 'If, as the century and the millennium slide to a close, our penal thinking is to be judged by the thinking which animates this Bill, then I, for one, will shrink from the judgment of history.'

Speaking immediately after Bingham, Lord Tebbit, a former minister in Mrs Thatcher's Cabinet, said that he had been concerned that several judges had made known their views on the Bill through radio and press reports. Lord Bingham had, in fact, made his views plain enough in his first routine press conference as Lord Chief Justice the previous October. Tebbit could understand the resentment of some judges about Parliamentary guidance, but said, 'I suppose it is a two-way street. If I may say so, there are a number of us in politics who have at times resented the extension of the doctrine of judicial review in the way that has happened in recent years.' He went on to say that 'as a result of those happenings, especially that of judges speaking so much in public outside this House' he now found it necessary in his role as a tabloid journalist to criticise the judicial conduct of judges in a way that he would not previously have thought to be proper. So far as the merits of the Bill were concerned, Tebbit thought that it addressed the growing loss of respect for the Bench in our country today.

As for the rest of the debate, twice as many peers spoke against the Bill as for it. The Bill's critics included Lord Woolf and Lord Donaldson, the present and former Masters of the Rolls, who could be added to the present and former Lord Chief Justices as opposing the government's scheme. Lord Carlisle of Bucklow spoke eloquently about the anomalies that would result from destroying the sentencing scheme that his committee had devised and

Lord Belstead, the chairman of the Parole Board and a former Conservative minister, explained[33] how the proposed abolition of the parole scheme 'could be a disastrous move for public safety' by doing away with risk assessments before the release of determinate-sentence prisoners.

During February and March 1997 the House of Lords considered the Bill in committee on five days, but we only need to consider two amendments that were made to it. The first was a Labour amendment moved by Lord McIntosh on 13 February. Its purpose was to give the courts some discretion on the mandatory sentences, but it did this in different ways for the life sentence for second-time violent offenders and the mandatory fixed terms for drug offenders and burglars. In the case of the life sentence, the effect of the amendment was only to provide that, in considering whether it was appropriate not to impose a life sentence (i.e., because there were exceptional circumstances) the court should have regard to the circumstances relating to either of the offences or to the offender. In the case of the mandatory fixed-term sentences, the amendment additionally required the court to have regard to the specific circumstances that would make the mandatory sentence 'unjust in all the circumstances'. It is not clear to the present authors why a distinction was carefully made in this way, so that the test of being 'unjust in all the circumstances' does not apply to the automatic life sentence, which is left with 'exceptional circumstances' as the only way out. Lord McIntosh explained[34] that the difference lay in the fact that in the case of the life sentence the trial judge would set the tariff and the Parole Board would determine risk and release, but that is not very convincing. On the face of it, the amended provision for automatic life sentences is open to virtually all the criticisms that Lord Bingham made of the original version in the second reading debate.

As Lord McIntosh's speech revealed, a major part of the Labour ploy was simply to draw Howard into the suppliant position of having to negotiate with Straw, as had happened a little earlier with a Lords amendment to require more judicial oversight of police bugging under the Police Bill. Howard was having none of that and accused Labour of trying to sneak in wrecking amendments in the Lords, having been too dishonest and cowardly to oppose the Bill openly in the Commons. Straw maintained in the 'On the Record' television programme that he wanted 'to see career burglars get tough minimum sentences, but I also want to see these introduced in a fair way . . . the way forward is for there to be discussions on this.'[35]

Lady Blatch opposed the amendments fiercely, emphasising her personal commitment to the proposition that a third-time domestic burglar should

---

[33] Ibid., col. 1019.
[34] Hansard HL, 13 February 1997, col. 334.
[35] *The Times*, 10 February 1997.

receive a sentence of at least three years under the Bill (equivalent to $4\frac{1}{2}$ years under current sentencing law) 'whether he steals a loaf of bread, a pint of milk or 50 pence from a purse'.[36] Several speakers had made it clear during the debates that there was no constitutional barrier to Parliament legislating to restrict judges' discretion as the Bill proposed, but Lady Blatch stated the doctrine of the supremacy of Parliament in a way that perhaps marks the extreme position in populist confrontation with the judiciary. 'I speak for the man on the top of the bus. There is another group of people whose views are paramount in these matters, not just senior judiciary. I am talking about the victims of crime and the public who look to Parliament for the right degree of protection set out in a framework to be implemented by the courts.'[37] The amendments were carried against the government by an alliance of Labour, the Liberal Democrats, unaligned peers, Law Lords and some Conservatives including former Cabinet ministers such as Lord Carlisle, Lord Belstead and the former Lord Chancellor, Lord Hailsham of St Marylebone. The vote was 180 to 172.

The other important amendments came on the government's initiative at the very last minute in response to the detailed exposure — mainly at the hands of Lord Belstead — of the layer upon layer of anomalies in the honesty in sentencing scheme. On 18 March Lady Blatch volunteered amendments reinstating a parole scheme under which prisoners serving three years or more would be eligible for release at five-sixths of the sentence on the recommendation of the Parole Board. In normal circumstances that would have seemed a major government retreat, but it came after the general election had been announced and was swamped by interest in the central question whether the Bill would be allowed to become law.

On 17 March Howard was taking the tough line that the Lords amendments to increase the courts' discretion to set aside mandatory sentences on burglars and drug offenders 'drove a coach and horses' through the Bill, and was insisting that it should go through unamended, on the grounds that Labour had not opposed the provision in the Commons.[38] When it came to the crunch in the Lords on 18 March, however, it was clear that there was a hard core of Liberal Democrat and unaligned peers who were prepared to go on mounting a filibuster to ensure that the Bill did not leave the Lords until the government promised not to overturn the crucial amendments in the Commons. Eventually the government threw in the towel and the filibustering peers let the Bill go back to the Commons in order to become law. The Liberal Democrats, however, briefed the press that Labour had sold out,[39] and

---

[36] Hansard HL, 13 February 1997, col. 356.
[37] Ibid., col. 355.
[38] *The Guardian*, 18 March 1997.
[39] *The Guardian*, 19 March 1997.

with their record of total opposition to the Bill they would doubtless have been prepared to block it completely if they had been given any support. A former Law Lord, Lord Bridge of Harwich, spoke in the Lords of a 'Satanic agreement' between the two front benches. Later, Alan Beith revealed in a letter to *The Independent* on 25 March that Labour would have been prepared to capitulate to Howard on deleting the crucial amendments, and that it was only at the Liberal Democrats' insistence that they had been retained.

In this way the Crime (Sentences) Act 1997 became law, with Labour disavowing the Conservative phantasmagoria of 'honesty' in sentencing, and with some judicial discretion inserted for the mandatory sentences. We can raise one cheer for the latter point, which manifestly improved this cynical piece of legislation, but it would be a great mistake to see it as sanitising the mandatory provisions. In the first place, the mandatory provision for life sentences remains virtually as arbitrary as it was in its original form and is bound to give rise to all the anomalies that flow from bad law. In the second place, all that had happened was that the mandatory determinate sentences had been turned into presumptive ones. This was immensely important from the point of view of the judges, who doubtless were genuinely repelled at the idea of being forced to pass sentences so unjust as to be anomalous. From the point of view of the overall effect on prison numbers, however, there is probably very little difference between a mandatory and a presumptive formula. In the understandable fixation about the issue of principle, this practical point received no attention at all.

Both of the main parties' election manifestos contained substantial sections on law and order. The Conservatives promised to reverse 'Labour's wrecking amendments to our tough Crime Bill' and repeated the claim that 'Prison works'. They supported this by asserting that 'Those sent to prison are less likely to reoffend on release than those given a community punishment', which repeated a claim made by David Maclean[40] on 24 March and was not in line with the Home Office statistical bulletin on the subject published on that day.[41] Labour undertook to 'implement an effective sentencing system for all the main offences to ensure greater consistency and stricter punishment for serious repeat offenders' and it promised that 'The Court of Appeal will have a duty to lay down sentencing guidelines for all the main offences'.

In the event, and despite the labyrinthine political preparations described in this chapter, law and order barely featured in the general election

---

[40] In *The Times*.

[41] The bulletin, 'Reconvictions of those Commencing Community Penalties in 1993', referred to the familiar statistical problem of late convictions for offences that were committed before community sentences were imposed. Allowing for that and other adjustments the bulletin concluded that the evidence suggested that 'there is currently no significant difference between reconviction rates for custody and all community penalties'.

campaign. Labour, who were generally reckoned to have established a lead on the topic, had adopted policies and tactics that enveloped the Conservative manoeuvres. Each party gave the subject one press conference but, as in the 1992 election, the topic never got off the ground and both parties seemed happy not to raise the profile of it.

THE ELEPHANT TRAP: COMMENT ON THE CRIME (SENTENCES) ACT 1997

Since the Crime (Sentences) Act 1997 has been so significant in setting the current political agenda, it is worth spelling out its implications quite fully.

The Conservative government's line boiled down to the propositions that the public needed more protection from dangerous and persistent criminals than the courts were currently providing, that serious and persistent criminals should be left in no doubt what would happen to them if they continued offending, that the public could not understand the arrangements for early release that the Criminal Justice Act 1991 had set up on the basis of the Carlisle committee report, and that the public and the police supported their proposals. A wide range of counter-arguments were deployed against the Bill, including the ideas that Lord Taylor had outlined in his lecture and all the points about American experience that we summarise at the end of chapter 5. These arguments are of very unequal weight. From our perspective, the fundamental points are as follows.

By its nature, mandatory minimum sentencing is a gross interference with the courts' ability to deal with different cases differently, according to the circumstances of the offence and the offender, and it is bound to be repugnant to any judiciary that prides itself on its commitment to fairness. That would be the case under any code of criminal law, but in this country the problem is particularly great. This is because it has become customary in English law-making to define criminal offences quite broadly, and to fix maximum penalties that are appropriate for the worst possible example of the offence in question, in the knowledge that the judge will be there to assess the seriousness of the offence and any mitigating factors.

American experience does seem to make it quite clear that mandatory minimum sentencing cannot be relied on for any special deterrent effect. It is also clear that once the device became adopted as a familiar kind of legislation in the USA, the political pressure to extend it to more and more offences became irresistible. The Crime (Sentences) Bill proposed a selection of offences for mandatory treatment partly on the grounds that they were ones about which the public felt particularly strongly, but they are certainly not the only offences of which that is true. If burglars should get mandatory

sentences, what about robbers, or vandals, or car thieves? Once a few
mandatory minima are adopted, the pressure for filling in the gaps between
offences with further mandatory minima is likely to mount inexorably.

In any event, even if new penalties are not laid down for other offences,
the implementation of mandatory minima is quite obviously bound to have
a knock-on effect. It is part of the judges' general responsibility to try to
maintain proportionality between sentences, and if the sentence for a
third-time domestic burglar were raised to 30 months in prison (the equivalent of a sentence of five years under current law) it is whimsically unrealistic
to suggest that the sentences for second-time domestic burglars or burglars
of commercial premises would remain unaffected, as the Conservative
government claimed to believe. The assertion in the White Paper that the
deterrent effect of mandatory sentences would reduce demand for prison
places by 20 per cent is also totally unsupported; the present authors do not
know where evidence to support such a proposition could be found in the
entire Western world. There are strict rules about the provision of accurate
information to Parliament, and no doubt the White Paper and the Bill's
explanatory and financial memorandum complied with them since their
costings were based on clearly stated assumptions. The assumptions were,
however, patently unrealistic, even on the proposition that it is possible to
phase in a major change in the severity of sentencing so that it would take
effect several years ahead without affecting sentencing practice in the
meantime.

That proposition is itself completely fanciful. Sentencers do not operate in
a mechanistic programmed way, and (as Brian Mawhinney had correctly
stated) they do not exist in a vacuum. Legislation as punitive as the Crime
(Sentences) Bill makes its own contribution to the severity of the climate.
The mathematical calculations of the legislation's effect in increasing
prisoner numbers up to a peak in 15 years' time simply do not reflect the real
world. What was happening in the real world as the Bill went through
Parliament was a record-breaking increase in the size of the prison population.
As regards the protection of the public, Lord Taylor was simply voicing
the virtually universal expert opinion when he said that there was no reason
to think that the government's proposals would achieve anything by way of
deterrence. The position on incapacitation is, we firmly believe, in line with
the general assessment we have set out in chapter 2. In particular, we do not
think that there is any reason to believe that concentrating on third-
time burglars would be so effective in identifying very high rate offenders
that it would displace the Tarling ratio of 25 per cent prison population
increase for 1 per cent crime reduction. In other words, if the entire project
were put into effect, there is every likelihood that the build-up of numbers
and expense would be faster and greater than the Conservative government's

estimates; the prison system would be overburdened and disrupted to an extreme degree; and the amount of crime would be shaved by no more than a very few percentage points.

The proposal of life sentences for serious second-time violent and sexual offenders warrants a special comment. Nobody would question the need to protect the public from dangerous offenders, but correctly identifying people who are likely to be seriously violent is extremely difficult and the Act's criteria of convictions from an arbitrary list of offences are extraordinarily crude. They would, to quote an example suggested by David Thomas, include the case of a man who was convicted at age 16 of consensual sexual intercourse with a girl of 12 and who was convicted of causing grievous bodily harm with intent in the course of a pub brawl 20 years later. An analysis of Parole Board reviews of prisoners serving determinate sentences for violent and sex offences showed that nine out of 10 of those considered the highest risk would not have been caught by the White Paper criteria, while one third of those who met the criteria were not considered dangerous.[42] It is right that more thought needs to be given to the old and difficult question of indeterminate sentencing for offenders who are judged to be particularly dangerous, but building a proposal on convictions from such an arbitrary list of offences is bound to produce wild anomalies.

The 'honesty in sentencing' provisions were probably the most obviously cobbled-together element of the Bill. The mechanics proposed for running the scheme in prisons were phenomenally complex and it is extremely hard to see how they could have operated fairly in practice. In considering the Bill's intentions, though, the significance of the 'honesty' provisions is their flagrant conflict with the rest of the Bill, as Lord Taylor explained in the House of Lords on 23 May 1996. This is not just a generalised criticism; it flows in a specific way from the effect of the mandatory sentences. Under the Bill's regime, for example, a third-time burglar would be sentenced to three years and have to serve 30 months, which is the minimum period to be served under current law by a prisoner sentenced to five years for, for example, an offence of rape that was sentenced at the bottom end of the scale. It is not conceivable that judges would be content to pass similar sentences for third-time burglary and for rape, so the Bill would inevitably create an unstable sentencing structure with an in-built tendency to push general sentencing levels higher.

Even if one were prepared to accept that the proposals for mandatory sentencing could have been put forward as a considered approach to crime control, the Crime (Sentences) Bill clearly contained the most extraordinary internal inconsistencies and the costing and phasing of its components was

---

[42] Hood, R. and Shute, S., 'Protecting the public: automatic life sentences, parole and high risk offenders', *Criminal Law Review* (1996), pp. 788–800.

specious. One experienced commentator[43] described the media as wanting 'to see if Labour was going to walk into what everyone acknowledges is a painstakingly prepared trap' and with the best will in the world it is impossible to see this legislation in any other way.

The Labour Party, of course, declined the invitation to fill a vacancy in the gaping elephant trap that Howard had prepared for them. We have noted that Jack Straw's position on 'honesty in sentencing' was a simple and practical counter-proposition on which his party could comfortably rest throughout the proceedings on the Bill. His commitment to progression in sentencing, on the other hand, seemed designed to outflank and go beyond the Conservative position by being capable of presentation as an even tougher response to repeat offenders than that which what was contained in Howard's White Paper. A sentencing scheme that was comprehensively progressive would, of course, have enormous implications. It would presumably require the replacement of the 1991 Act, which still makes offence seriousness the main criterion of sentencing, notwithstanding the special provisions for incapacitatory sentences on violent and sexual offenders and the ambiguities of the amended section 29 in respect of previous convictions. It would endorse the idea of a 'ladder' of sentences that would inexorably lead through the various community punishments to prison, no matter how demanding the community punishments might be. Its implications for the prison population would self-evidently be huge.

In the light of all this we can see that a similar proposition was concealed in both the Conservative and Labour positions on the Crime (Sentences) legislation. This was that the current, seriousness-based, sentencing regime should be discarded and replaced by some new version of the nineteenth-century cumulative principle. That would be the obvious consequential effect through the system if high mandatory sentences were put in place for repeat convictions of common offences such as domestic burglary; and it was overtly advocated by the proposals on progression in Straw's paper. Neither party stated the full implications and costs of its policies, however. The Conservatives maintained that their proposals were limited to a few carefully selected offences, and they produced the unrealistic costings that we have described. The Labour Party took a position within a generalised statement of intention which contained no details and costings whatsoever. So far as Labour's stance on the Bill was concerned, they had found a flexible position that enabled them easily to accept the proposed mandatory sentences, resources permitting, but also to imply that their own response to repeat offenders would be something altogether more comprehensive than mandatory minima for a handful of offences chosen at random.

---

[43] Gibbon, G. 'Reporting the Crime Bill', *Howard Journal of Criminal Justice* (February 1997).

With the two major political parties taking these convergent positions, the whole question of crime and sentencing policy sank to a low level of interest in the media, apart from the odd cartoon at the expense of the newly found punitivism of Labour policies. It is head-on political confrontation between the party heavyweights in the House of Commons that attracts continuing attention, and that was not going to be on offer. In terms of neutralising the topic as a campaign issue, the Labour policy was to be completely successful.

One feature which stands out a mile from the story of the 'law and order counter-reformation' is the extent to which the 1991 Act policies were systematically repudiated, so that the 1990 and 1996 White Papers are symmetrically opposed in very many ways. Where the 1991 Act was painfully prepared by consultation and discussion papers over a couple of years, the contents of the Crime (Sentences) Bill were announced fully fledged at the Conservative Party conference. Where the 1990 White Paper stabilised the parole scheme, the 1996 White Paper dashed it to pieces, notwithstanding the consequent loss of public protection. Where the 1990 White Paper set out the range of factors implied by its title of *Crime, Justice and Protecting the Public*, the 1996 White Paper ostentatiously occupied a single-issue campaigning position of professed concern for public protection that did not fit well with the ending of parole. Where the 1990 White Paper earnestly explained the reasons for restraint in the use of imprisonment, the 1996 White Paper viewed increased use of prison with enthusiasm.

Does this marked polarity between the 1990 and 1996 policies reflect some deeper evolution of the politics of punishment in this country, similar to what has happened in the USA? And is it useful to see a common thread of theoretical thinking between the American and British experiences, with benignly conceived retribution theory leading in practice to an escalation of severity?

To answer the second question first, we doubt if the 1990 White Paper's assertion of a 'just deserts' philosophy has in any real sense formed a conceptual bridge to the populist punitivism of its 1996 successor. The 1991 Act's perceived weakness and its repudiation by the judiciary were part of the background against which the Major administration formed the policies with which it went into the general election, but the 1993 U-turn was specific to the Major government's situation and it does not mean that British and American penal policy went through the same evolutionary course. This country has never institutionalised the treatment model in the form of such extensive indeterminate sentencing as existed in the USA, and it seems to us that it was the shift to determinate sentencing that was probably crucial in the American story. Having said that, there is, as always, an American dimension to what has happened here. To put it crudely, the 1990 White Paper must now be seen as mistaken in thinking that there was much in the way of practical American precedent at that time for the sort of liberal offence-based approach that it advocated. Howard's 1995 party conference speech, on the other hand, had a confident grasp of the main features of populist American law-making, and knew exactly how to package these ready-made devices into a politically powerful message.

It is that politicisation and populism that provide the answer to the first question. By now it is obvious that the events since 1993 mark a step change both in British imprisonment and in the political discourse. Howard's assertion that 'Prison works', the blatant American ancestry of the Crime (Sentences) Bill, and the acceptance of mandatory sentencing by both the main political parties in the House of Commons are extraordinary things to have happened. The courts' use of imprisonment has behaved in a way that is just as extraordinary, so that the prison population has gone up by around 40 per cent since the 'Prison works' speech. In only four years high sentencing has taken root in the courts and in bipartisan politics. The history of what has happened in the USA shows how very difficult it is to break out of this spiral.

PART 3

CURRENT POLICY AND PROSPECTS FOR THE FUTURE

11 A New Kind of Crisis

THE POISONED CHALICE

There were many factors at work in the 'law and order counter-reformation' of 1993. They included the high levels of recorded crime in previous years, the collapse of confidence in the Conservative government, the repositioning of the Labour Party on crime policy, and the intense campaign in the media. However, the essential point to grasp is that 1993 was also the only short period for at least 30 years in which the prison population has been in balance with accommodation. At any time between the early 1960s and the early 1990s even the harshest Home Secretary would have found it difficult to drum up custom and announce that he did not flinch from the prospect of more prisoners. Nobody in the prison world doubts the truth of Sir Alexander Paterson's dictum that 'Wherever prisons are built, courts will make use of them' and prison building programmes have often been opposed precisely because they are likely to stimulate high sentencing by the courts. Indeed, the Home Office Permanent Secretary who presided over the formulation of the 1980s building programme commented in 1989 that, while that pro-gramme was scheduled to provide 21,000 extra places, 'We all know that extending prison capacity is the necessary solution which never quite solves the problem'.[1] Even the most world-weary observer, however, would have found it hard to imagine that within months of the achievement of a reasonable balance between court demand and prison resources there would be an unprecedented campaign by the government itself to whip up the

---

[1] Cubbon, Sir B., 'Prison policy and practice', *Prison Service Journal* (1989), p. 57.

severity of sentencing, with the totally predictable result of creating the
present developing crisis four years later.

If, as happened in 1993, the government of the day parades its insouciance
about the prospect of gross overloading of the prison system for which it is
directly responsible, it is extraordinarily difficult for an opposition party with
electoral ambitions to appear much more tender towards offenders than the
government itself. Also, the fact must be faced that the history of unsuccess-
ful attempts at sentencing reform prior to the 1993 'law and order counter-
reformation' makes it that much more difficult to revisit the question of
placing sentencing under any kind of restraint. On the ground, sentencing is
still being driven by the first fine careless rapture of 'Prison works', despite
the increasingly clearly damaging effects on the prison system. It is hard to
imagine more difficult circumstances for sensible decision-making about the
use of imprisonment.

An increase of 57 per cent in the prison population in five years, during
which the number of convictions for indictable offences has appreciably
fallen, should be seen as something that has gone seriously wrong, not as a
balanced approach to punishment and crime control. There is now a glimmer
of hope that the present tide of imprisonment will not be accepted as the
beginning of a radically more severe imprisonment policy as we go into the
new millennium, but the signs are still difficult to read. In this chapter we
explain why there is a need to build in some machinery to make the criminal
justice system more stable and to reduce the chances of such violent surges.
Without that, we risk lurching several further steps towards the costly and
destructive world of American prisons.

HOW WE GOT HERE

If this short book shows anything it is that, in addition to being a gut issue
with the capacity for huge public and political charge, the subject of
imprisonment involves an intractable mix of quasi-constitutional, symbolic
and economic issues.

To recapitulate, by the late 1970s prison overcrowding was routinely
running at a level that had scandalous effects on the entire prison system.
Everyone, including the judiciary, joined in the ritual condemnation of this
situation but the pressure of numbers continued to grow. Something had to
give, and in the circumstances it is not so very surprising that there should
have been pressure from all sides to expand the safety valve of parole to a
greater extent than it could bear. (Whether Leon Brittan's restrictions on
parole for serious offenders must be seen as the inevitable political accom-
paniment of that expansion is another matter.) The reduction of the minimum

qualifying period for parole in 1984 only brought the prison system relief for a few months, however, and when the new arrangements' bizarre effects on sentences soon became apparent, the judiciary's sympathy for government interest in sentencing reform apparently sank to a new level of scepticism. That must have influenced the course of later events. Meanwhile, the build-up of long-term prisoners was sharply encouraged by the Brittan restrictions.

Against all the odds, the Carlisle committee managed to come up with a coherent scheme that stabilised the parole and early release system. The Criminal Justice Act 1991 did get that issue right. Its codification of probation and other non-custodial disposals was also long overdue; the recognition that community punishments had to be made more credible to the sentencers was surely correct; and the linkage between fines and ability to pay must have been right in principle. But the central concern of the Act's framers was to establish a framework of desert-based principles for sentencing in the belief that this would simultaneously lead to more consistency and less imprisonment. In the event, the Act was so vulnerable on its treatment of previous convictions, multiple offences and unit fines, the Major administration was so rapid in its repudiation of those elements, and the judiciary were so ineffective in defining the custody threshold that the Act has been left as a stranded wreck that warns of the dangers of venturing in these waters.

The repudiation of the provisions on previous convictions etc. in 1993 now emerges clearly as the crossover point when sentencers, media and both main political parties were all more or less in the same place at the same time,[2] and the prison population was in balance with the accommodation. However, this moment of equilibrium was simply the result of volatile processes happening to coincide, and the underlying instability was as great as ever. As it was, the course of events was played out against the background of the febrile media climate on crime in the aftermath of the Bulger murder, which must have influenced the then government's frenzied reaction to the Labour Party's recognition that it needed to reposition itself on law and order. The die was cast at the party conferences in September and October 1993 with Michael Howard's 'Prison works' rejoinder to Tony Blair's claim that 'Labour is the party of law and order in Britain today'. From that point on there was a race by the then government to establish a more extreme law and order position than the Labour Party, whose refusal to be typecast as the befrienders of criminals left a vacuum into which the judiciary were drawn.

The passage of the Crime (Sentences) Act in 1997 saw the Conservative government castigating the judges for having views less punitive than those

---

[2] Ashworth, A. and Hough, M., 'Sentencing and the climate of opinion', *Criminal Law Review* (1996), p. 776.

that the government attributed to the 'man on the top of the bus', while in the real world outside Westminster the severity of sentencing was actually sending the prison population spiralling up to the maximum safe level. This episode was like a bad dream. But it represented the real situation immediately before the general election and it is still powerful in setting the agenda.

The events since 1982, beginning with the government lunging after any device to keep the prison population down, and ending with it straining every nerve to push the population up, do not fit any single explanation. Clearly, one way of analysing them is as a struggle for power between the government and the judiciary, and Andrew Ashworth has already made a start with that approach in a lecture[3] in which he cogently argues that the judiciary's central concern has simply been to maintain maximum sentencing discretion and repel any attempts at interference. Ashworth draws attention, for example, to the inconsistency between the judges' determination to maintain deterrence as a sentencing objective in 1993 and their pouring scorn on the notion of deterrence in the context of the Crime (Sentences) Act 1997. He also points out that it was the mandatory quality of the government's proposals in 1995, rather than the idea of severe sentencing as such, that seems to have excited the judges' special animosity. There is plainly a good deal of truth in that analysis, but it also has to be recognised that the successive interventions by government over the years all contained much that was ill-judged and defective. The judges may indeed deserve some of Ashworth's strictures, but if their 'Leave it to us' attitude has been one half of the problem they can also be forgiven for thinking that the government did not have all the answers either.

The confrontation between the judges and the Major administration over control of sentencing policy was set in the context of a much wider struggle over the proper role of the judiciary. That certainly coloured some of the incidents that we have recorded, as was made clear in one of the exchanges in the House of Lords during the passage of the Crime (Sentences) Bill. We are not equipped to go into all that background, which involves the judges' participation in political debate, theoretical speculation whether there could be a boundary to the ultimate supremacy of Parliament, and apparent resentment by the previous government of certain judgments in judicial review cases.[4] For our purpose it is sufficient to note that the developing wrangle on sentencing policy took place against that background and was itself an important field of battle in the wider warfare. What is important

---

[3] Ashworth, A., 'Sentencing in the 80s and 90s: the Struggle for Power', the Eve Saville Memorial Lecture, 21 May 1997, London: Institute for the Study and Treatment of Delinquency, 1997.

[4] For a synopsis, see Rozenberg, J., *Trial of Strength* (London: Richard Cohen Books, 1997).

from the limited perspective of this book is simply the destabilising effect that the high sentencing campaign from 1993 seems to have had on the courts. The familiar question of getting the right balance between Parliamentary control of sentencing policy and judicial discretion at the point of delivery must have been made far more intractable by the perception of a deliberate campaign to undermine public confidence in the sentencers.

This raises the whole question of public opinion. On the one hand, there have been many opinion poll findings apparently revealing the widespread view that offenders are inadequately punished. On the other hand, there is a mounting body of evidence that respondents are typically ill-informed about the actual level of sentencing and that there is quite a high correlation between such misconceptions and punitive attitudes. Where people are well-informed, the level of agreement with sentencing practice has been shown to be significant. A study of 2,300 jurors, for example, found that 46 per cent thought the sentences in their cases were at least as severe as they expected, compared with only 23 per cent who thought the sentences too lenient.[5]

Public misconceptions about sentencing exist alongside difficulties in measuring true levels of crime. One of the most important sources of information on crime in this country is the government's own biennial British Crime Survey (BCS), which is based on interviews with 16,500 respondents. All experts agree that this supplies an important corrective to the traditional figures for crime recorded by the police, since it is not subject to the considerable variations in the rate at which people report crime to the police, and the rate at which the police record crimes that are reported to them. The 1996 White Paper began by noting that, thanks to the efforts of the police, recorded crime had fallen dramatically in the previous three years, and it went on to state the government's full belief that 'Prison works'. Very little public attention was ever given to the BCS figures, published later in 1996, which showed offences *rising* by 2 per cent between 1993 and 1995.[6] The truth of the matter is almost certainly that the recorded crime figures have been greatly affected by the imposition of performance standards on the police, and the effect this had in making the police (very understandably) reluctant to record crimes that were unlikely to be cleared up.

We do not believe that any sound reason has been shown for thinking that the crime rate since 1993 has been linked to the level of imprisonment by anything more than the very weak linkage that can usually be expected, which we described in chapter 2. The last government frequently presented the two things with the implication of a much closer alignment than that,

---

[5] Zander, M. and Henderson, P., *Crown Court Study* (Royal Commission on Criminal Justice Research Study No. 19) (London: HMSO, 1993).
[6] 'The 1996 British Crime Survey', *Home Office Statistical Bulletin*, 19/96.

however. Immediately before the general election, for example, Michael Howard presented the recorded crime figures for 1996 by insisting that there was a 'clear relationship' between a sharply rising prison population and falling crime.[7] Very small variations in reconviction figures were also seized on to support the argument that prison was the most effective way of preventing reoffending, and we noted in chapter 10 that the Conservative election manifesto made claims about this that were at variance with the Home Office's own research findings. We cannot judge how far these things have registered with the public. What is clear, though, is that from 1993 there were four years of British politics in which there was increasingly close alignment between the two major political parties in the encouragement of higher imprisonment. The previous government's claims for the crime control effects of prison largely went by default. On the other hand, the Labour Party's method of retort, by holding the then government directly accountable for the doubling of recorded crime since 1979, may have strengthened the equally misleading notion that crime is susceptible to direct government control. The general movement of crime figures in recent years seems, in fact, to have been broadly in line with the proposition put forward in a Home Office research study in 1990 that property crime tends to rise in times of economic recession and to fall in boom periods, while violent crime moves in exactly the opposite way and is closely linked with levels of beer consumption.[8] However one interprets events since 1993, the public have certainly not been given much reason to think that there is any limit to the supply of punishment that can be delivered.

By the beginning of 1997 the relations between the then government and the judiciary had reached an intolerable nadir, the prisons were back in an accommodation crisis, and the political rivalry to appear tough was in full spate. That was the background to some proposals for a Royal Commission on Crime and Punishment that were made by Sir Louis Blom-Cooper QC and Professor Sean McConville in a Prison Reform Trust pamphlet published in January 1997.

Blom-Cooper and McConville argued that national policy on crime and punishment had become deeply confused under the stream of political rhetoric, and that there would be great advantage in removing it from political contention. They believed that the American experience (which they saw as beginning to happen here) showed that once these issues become the subject of party political contention it becomes impossible for politicians to accept that government has very limited options in these matters, and that what is needed is a kind of indemnity for politicians, which for the time

---

[7] *The Guardian*, 18 March 1997.

[8] 'Notifiable Offences, England and Wales, July 1996 to June 1997', *Home Office Statistical Bulletin*, 23/97; Field, S., *Trends in Crime and their Interpretation: a Study of Recorded Crime in Post-War England and Wales* (Home Office Research Study No.119) (London: HMSO, 1990).

being allows them to suspend judgment and refrain from denunciation. They therefore proposed a Royal Commission with terms of reference that would cover the entire field of the causes and prevention of crime, the efficacy of the criminal justice system, the scope of the criminal law, dispute resolution, the principles of sentencing, public confidence, and the organisation and funding of criminal justice research.

We think that Blom-Cooper and McConville hit the nail on the head with their description of the problems that have been caused by the recent style of political handling of crime and punishment issues. Like them, we think that the American parallels for what has been happening here are far too close for comfort. Their prescription for defusing the situation does, however, reflect more faith than we have in the ability of a Royal Commission to reach agreement on such extremely wide issues. We also doubt whether politicians of the parties that had stimulated the present situation could find it in themselves to exercise a self-denying ordinance on the issue for several years. In any event, the essence of the proposal was that a Royal Commission should be set up at the very outset of the new Parliament in 1997, and it is clear that the government are going down a different path. However, we do think that Blom-Cooper and McConville must be absolutely right in saying that there should be a better machinery than currently exists for producing disinterested and authoritative reports on a limited number of urgent matters, and we return to that point at the end of this chapter.

A CRISIS IN THE MAKING

Writers on prisons customarily engage in a dialogue with themselves about whether the prisons can be said to be in a state of crisis and, if so, what kind of crisis. In the 1980s it was easy to diagnose a crisis on many dimensions, since the system was quite evidently near breakdown and many of the shortcomings identified in the Woolf report were glaringly obvious. It would be untrue and unhelpful to say that the present situation is just the same. The post-Woolf changes were very great improvements, notwithstanding subsequent modifications, and the level of overcrowding 10 years ago was significantly worse than now. (In July 1987, when Douglas Hurd introduced half remission for short-sentence prisoners, the prison population was 51,000 in accommodation for 41,700. The figures for October 1997 were about 63,000 in accommodation for 57,000.) Nevertheless, it does seem more likely than not that the prison system is now moving into a new kind of crisis — a manufactured crisis of excessive numbers being poured into a prison system with much increased security and control capability.

For the purposes of this book there is no need to go into the twists and turns of prison finance from 1993 to the general election. The main points are the rapidly escalating prison population, so that by the end of the period population forecasts became manifestly obsolete as soon as they were made; the need to accommodate substantial spending on security following the Woodcock and Learmont reports; and the imposition in 1995 of severe cuts on running costs. Against that background the Labour election manifesto noted that the prison service faced serious financial problems and undertook to audit the resources available.

The audit, which was unusually frank and informative, was published just before the Parliamentary summer recess on 25 July 1997, when Jack Straw told the House of Commons in a written answer that its main findings were:

(a)   The prison population had risen by 17,000 or nearly 40 per cent in the four years to June, and had increased by 2,440 (the equivalent of four average prisons) in the three months since the general election. That was 1,600 more than the forecast made in April.

(b)   The previous government's building programme was already being outstripped by the rise in numbers, which were now forecast to exceed the maximum capacity of the prisons later in 1997 and would do so again by a larger margin by early 1999.

(c)   The number of prisoners 'doubled' — held two to a cell designed for one — had increased from 7,251 in 1992 to 10,926 at the end of June and, on current plans, would probably increase to around 16,000 by early 1999.

(d)   Purposeful activity had nearly dropped to the 1992 level, limiting the scope for reducing the risk of prisoners reoffending on release.

The operational maximum capacity figure is a 'soft' one that is based on an assessment of both physical capacity and additional risks to control and security, which are affected by staffing levels and the facilities that are available. In parallel with the audit, the Home Office was authorised to spend £43 million on 290 extra prisoner places and additional staffing and funding for regime activities. Nevertheless, the audit's core finding remains that, on the then population forecast, the number of prisoners would be within the maximum safe level for most of 1998 but would then exceed it by an increasing margin.

Douglas Hurd was forced to take action in 1987 when the prison population was 9,300 above the certified accommodation. The July audit showed that overcrowding was forecast to be at that level in the summer of 1999, and would reach 11,500 — that is, the equivalent of 23 medium-sized prisons — in 2001–2. Even these figures do not reflect the full seriousness of the situation: the prison service needs a margin of accommodation above the certified figure in order to cope properly with operational demands, and the Treasury have agreed that this margin should be 5 per cent. On 13 February 1998 Straw announced a further package of emergency finance, to provide 3,920 places at a cost of £70 million.

Addressing the other side of the accommodation equation, Straw had announced on 20 November 1997[9] that the government proposed to take power in the forthcoming Crime and Disorder Bill to release selected prisoners under home detention curfews, to be enforced by electronic tagging. This arrangement, subject to a risk assessment in each case, would be available on a sliding scale for prisoners serving between three months and four years. The shortest period of tagging would be two weeks and the longest two months.

While any relief to the prisons is obviously welcome, this proposal is self-evidently a safety valve that demonstrates just how far out of balance the criminal justice system has become. There is something badly wrong in a situation in which more and more offenders are shoved into prison at one end, while the government exercises every ingenuity to invent cumbersome ways of letting them out early at the other. That is more or less where we were in the early 1980s, when the pressure to do something about prison overcrowding distorted decision-making on the sensible limits of parole.

If home detention orders were granted to half those eligible, the reduction of the prison population would be about 3,000, which is less than the growth in the population between May and November 1997. The problem is clearly much more serious than that. Unless and until there is a radical change in the input–accommodation equation it is very hard to see that the situation can be any better than one of steady deterioration, with the prison service improvising just enough to survive, management control of systems weakening as they become overstretched, and prisoners' regimes being steadily eroded.

The very latest Home Office prison population projections[10] depart from the previous methodology and display three projections made on completely different assumptions. The highest of these — resulting in a figure of 90,100 in 2004/5 — assumes the extraordinary imprisonment rate of over 90 per cent in the Crown Court, while the lowest — resulting in 64,300 in 2004/5 — assumes that the position will effectively stabilise through demographic factors alone. We acknowledge that it is extremely difficult to make accurate predictions in this field, and there is no point in our adding our own guess. We would only say that the safest assumption must surely be that, in the absence of focused intervention, there will be a continuation of significant growth.

SENTENCING AND THE SENTENCERS

It is a truism that no part of the criminal justice system can be fully understood without an understanding of the other parts, and it is also a truism

[9] Hansard HC, 20 November 1997, col. 453.
[10] Revised projections of long term trends, in the prison population to 2005 *Home Office Statistical Bulletin*, 2/98 London: Home Office, 1998.

that sentencing should not be held accountable for choices that are made elsewhere, simply because the passing of sentence is the only decision along the line that takes place fully in the open. In the present developing crisis all the evidence indicates that an unprecedented change has taken place at the sentencing level, and that changes elsewhere in the system are much less significant.

The level of recorded crime has fallen in each year since 1992 (though, as noted above, the figures for violent offences are rising and those for property offences falling in a way that is probably associated with the performance of the economy). The police clear-up rate has hardly changed during the period, at around 26 per cent. The number prosecuted in the courts for indictable offences has fallen slightly, from 560,000 in 1993 to 551,000 in 1996, and the number found guilty in those years has similarly dropped from 306,000 to 300,000. Both those last figures are well down on the numbers for 1985, when the number of convictions for indictable offences was 441,700.

All these changes are virtually irrelevant in comparison with the rise in the courts' use of imprisonment. To spell it out, the imprisonment rate for indictable offences in the Crown Court slowly sank from rather below 55 per cent in 1985 to 48 per cent in the penultimate quarter of 1992, immediately before the Criminal Justice Act 1991 came into force. It then dropped to 42 per cent by the end of the year, but immediately bounced back to reach 52 per cent by the time of the amendments to the 1991 Act in July 1993. After rising to settle down slightly below the 1985 level throughout 1994, it rose to 56 per cent in 1995 and then stabilised at over 60 per cent in 1996, its highest level since 1954, and nearly half as much again as the figure at the end of 1992. In the magistrates' courts the pattern was even more pronounced, with the imprisonment rate doubling from 4.8 per cent in 1992 to 9.6 per cent in 1996. The combined rate for all courts in 1996 was 21.6 per cent, the highest figure since before 1948.

Increasing the imprisonment rate means sucking more offenders into prison for less serious offences, with the result that the average sentence length is normally pulled down. In the current punitive cycle that is not what is happening, and average sentences in the Crown Court have increased for almost all indictable offence groups. So the courts are not only sending more people to prison but they are also sending them there for much longer. This is an extraordinary thing to happen.

The larger number of long sentences may, in fact, be having the most significant impact on the prisons, with the number of adult males serving sentences in the range 12 months to four years increasing by 11 per cent between 1995 and 1996, and the number serving more than four years going up by 10 per cent. So the trend towards longer sentences through the 1980s and 1990s is still continuing in full spate. There does not appear to be any special factor in the mix of cases going to the courts, or any change in relevant legislation during the period, that could possibly explain a shift of the magnitude that has occurred. In so far as cautioning practice is relevant it ought to have had the effect of diluting the mix of cases that went to trial, since the cautioning rate fell slightly throughout the period.

The truth is that the courts are using prison more freely than at any time in living memory, and they are also passing much longer sentences than would have been considered normal 20 or 30 years ago. The explosion of prison numbers is due to an absolutely extraordinary step change in sentencing norms over a very short period. To make matters worse, the remand population (which decreased by nearly 1,000 from 1994 to 1996) is now also rising steadily.

It is implicit in this account that the sentencing surge has been mainly attributable to the politics of a particular situation and that sentencers have been responding to the knowledge that nobody would stand up for them if they were reviled in the media. The judges' own opinions of the causes behind shifts in sentencing are usually shrouded in mystery. On this occasion, however, the Lord Chief Justice, Lord Bingham of Cornhill, has put his views on the record in two important speeches.[11]

In Lord Bingham's opinion the higher rate of custodial sentencing and increased length of sentences cannot be explained by changes in sentencing powers and is simply due to 'the vocal expression of opinion by influential public figures that custody is an effective penalty'. Judges and magistrates had been the subject of criticism 'none the less influential because indirect — for imposing what are widely portrayed as excessively lenient sentences' and that view had been strongly supported in 'certain sections of the media'. As a result, magistrates and judges had increasingly been choosing custody in the middle rank of cases where there was a choice to be made between custody and a community punishment, and Lord Bingham was forthright in saying that he regarded this trend as 'a real source for concern' on grounds of both justice and effectiveness.

In Lord Bingham's view the problem that the courts have in using community penalties instead of imprisonment is partly due to a lack of confidence about them in the mind of the public and the perception of the media. Probation officers should be demanding taskmasters, but they were not seen in that light by the public. This question of public perception should, he said, be vigorously addressed, though it was a political rather than a judicial task to convince the public that community punishments were not a soft option.

---

[11] Bingham, Lord, 'The Sentence of the Court', Police Foundation Lecture, 10 July 1997; and speech to the National Probation Convention 12 November 1997, both Lord Chancellor's Department Press Office.

WHERE WE ARE GOING

As this book was being written the new government's policies on crime were flooding out in a series of announcements that go far wider than our concern with prisons. They include action to reform the Crown Prosecution Service, enormously wide-ranging proposals for the reform of the youth justice system, and action to attack delays in the criminal justice process. From our point of view there are two vitally important things. The first is the emphasis that the government is clearly going to give to the development of new regimes of community intervention, since these obviously have the potential of diverting offenders from custody and tackling offending in more positive ways. The second is the proposed new function for the Court of Appeal, to which we shall return at the end of this chapter.

Amidst all the activity, the outlines of a somewhat new approach to the use of prison may be beginning to emerge. In the area of youth crime the government has come forward with wide-ranging proposals for the reduction of offending in which custody only forms one component.[12] More generally, the government's pronouncements have increasingly reflected a real understanding of prisons and of how counter-productive it is to crowd them beyond their capacity. The Labour election manifesto included an undertaking to ensure that 'prison regimes are constructive and require inmates to face up to their offending behaviour', and there is no reason to doubt the importance that the government attaches to that. On 20 November 1997[13] Jack Straw drew attention to the fact that 'If regimes are heavily overcrowded, they are less likely to be constructive' and he pointed to the existence of clear research evidence[14] that the reoffending rate is higher in those circumstances. His conclusion that 'an increase in the reoffending rate as a result of locking people up is not a sensible way to protect the public' struck a note that had not been heard from either front bench for some years.

On the other hand, there is a heavy legacy of policy conceived in the period leading up to the general election, in the wake of the increasingly harsh policies of the previous government. This is clearest in the context of the Crime (Sentences) Act 1997, on which Straw announced the new government's decisions on 30 July. As expected, the Act's 'honesty in sentencing' provisions were then finally put to bed, and Straw confirmed that the government would instead require courts to explain the effects of

---

[12] *No More Excuses; a New Approach to Tackling Youth Crime in England and Wales* (Cm 3809) (London: HMSO, 1997).

[13] Hansard HC, 20 November 1997, col. 459.

[14] Probably Farrington, D.P. and Nuttall, C.P., 'Prison Size; Overcrowding, Prison Violence and Recidivism', *Journal of Criminal Justice*, vol. 8 pp. 221–231 (1980).

sentences at the time they were passed. The mandatory life sentences for repeat violent offenders and presumptive seven-year sentences for repeat drug traffickers were to be brought into force on 1 October. The presumptive three-year sentence for third-time domestic burglars, however, was to be left on the shelf for the time being, and the government would consider implementing it only in the light of resources and the prison service's capacity. Later, on 24 November, Straw confirmed that on the question of third-time domestic burglars the new government's 'position is exactly that of the previous government. They willed the end, but failed to will the means.'

Straw thus sidestepped the worst landmine in the Crime (Sentences) Act 1997 by implementing only the two categories of prescribed sentences that would not involve large numbers of extra prisoners. That would enable him to say that he had redeemed the Labour manifesto's promise of stricter punishment for serious repeat offenders, and perhaps that is where that particular matter will end. His attitude to the Act's three-year sentences for third-time burglars, however, was founded simply and solely on the likelihood (or, rather, unlikelihood) of adequate resources being available. The new government's attitude to such sentences presumably remains one of thorough approval in principle. The government will constantly be reminded of this professed policy ideal, and it is simply impossible to see how it can be squared with any realistic approach towards the more restrained use of prison. The Labour government showed a similar reluctance to distance itself from the Crime (Sentences) Act when, in February 1998, it refused to accept an amendment to remove wounding with intent from the list of offences that triggered the mandatory life sentence, despite having consistently argued for that during the passage of the legislation.[15]

There is therefore a deep ambivalence in the government's posture, and the ultimate question for the prisons is whether in these circumstances a sufficiently clear message to influence the sentencers' use of prison is likely to emerge.

The government's overall game plan — like that of so many previous administrations — is clearly going to depend on repackaging community punishments and presenting them as both being more demanding and providing more public protection. Straw has repeatedly stressed that he will not ask the courts to lower their use of custody, but that if community punishments are improved, they may command more confidence both with the public and with sentencers. On the Radio 4 programme 'The World This Weekend' on 13 July 1997, for example, he said, 'Public confidence in community sentences is lower in this country than it is in many comparable

---

[15] Hansard HL, 24 February 1998, col. 611.

European countries. If we can improve the effectiveness of community sentences, make them tougher, then sentencers will feel better about using them.'

Trying to tempt sentencers to use new or improved non-custodial sentences in preference to prison has inevitably been the normal approach to the problem of an unmanageable prison population for at least the last four decades. As a result, the courts in this country already have an unusually large range of community penalties available to them, and they have in fact been making increasing use of them. The problem is that much of this increased use reflects a drastic decline in the use of the fine, which has fallen by half in the last 10 years. Punishment has been pushed up the scale — away from the fine and into community punishment and prison, both of which suffered financial cuts in the last years of the previous government. To get the country's punishment system into a sensible alignment with the resources that are likely to be available would therefore need a more wide-ranging adjustment than simply diverting a proportion of custodial sentencing into community punishments. What is required is a wider shift of court disposals down the ladder of punishment, and that may be an extremely difficult thing to do against the expectations that have been generated for both punishment and public protection. We need to be aware of that wider background, though it is only the top part of the punishment scale that concerns us here.

By now it seems likely that there will be three main elements to the way in which community punishments are relaunched. One element, exactly as in the Conservative 1991 project, will be renewed emphasis on better organisation of the probation service, compliance with national standards, and insistence that community penalties are a form of punishment. The other elements will depend on new technology and know-how. On 20 November Straw announced that the previous government's trials of electronic tagging had proved highly successful, making it 'clear that the technology can offer substantial benefits for victims and the public'.[16] The trials were to be extended, but it was perfectly clear that the government was sufficiently persuaded that tagging could be one way of increasing confidence in community sentences, and this is bound to become a major new selling point. The final element is likely to be the institutionalised adoption of modern techniques of offending behaviour control, in the light of the Chief Inspector of Probation's report on what works in probation supervision, due in the first half of 1998.

It is now possible to see the outline of the way in which the government may hope that the developing prison crisis can be kept under control, within

---

[16] Hansard HC, 20 November 1997, col. 454.

the timescale up to the next general election. For most of 1998 the prison population is forecast to be within the maximum usable capacity of the system, because of the new accommodation that is coming on stream during the period. In 1999 the new home detention orders would begin to deliver their 3,000-place reduction in the population, the Febuary 1998, £70 million package will be providing places, and new community punishments would be on offer to sentencers, with a potentially potent mixture of electronic tagging and crisply organised delivery of courses on the control of offending behaviour. Nevertheless, the present surge in sentencing is on such a massive scale, and the past encouragement of harsh attitudes has been so pronounced, that there can be no confidence that a careful policy on these lines will be enough to keep the prison crisis in bounds. In the current climate there is bound to be very great difficulty in establishing *any* community penalties as providing sufficient control and public protection. Even if the current bundle of policies is sufficient to keep the prison show on the road until the time of the next general election, it is hardly calculated to confront the deep problems being created by a high imprisonment policy in the longer term.

It is sometimes suggested that the costs of prison expansion are so high, and the rigour of the government's commitment to its public expenditure targets is so total, that this discipline alone will force an early change of policy. We are not so sure about that. The emergency funding of £43 million and £70 million already show how, even at the height of the government's post-election financial rectitude, quite large sums of money can uncannily be found when there is a sufficiently compelling reason. The previous government found £120.6 million rising to £283.8 million for prisons in its final budget. Historically, law and order services have always done better for public expenditure than the rest of Whitehall thinks they deserve, and the political reasons that lie behind that may not have changed all that much with the change of government.

In the past a major constraint on providing prison accommodation was the heavy up-front cost of paying for construction costs at the time they were incurred, so that the Whitelaw building programme which was eventually expanded to yield 21 prisons cost around £1.2 billion on top of operating costs. All that has changed with the Private Finance Initiative (PFI), under which new privately built and operated prison facilities do not present a charge to the government until places are available for occupation. Whatever Labour leaders may have said before the general election about running prisons for profit, it is now clear that the PFI route is 'the only game in town' for construction projects of this kind, and that it gets the job done far more quickly than had been customary under public-sector provision. That much is implicit in the fact that Straw has approved four privately built and operated prisons. We are not suggesting that provision is likely to be forthcoming for an expensive new policy commitment such as the third-time burglar provisions of the Crime (Sentences) Act 1997, but meeting the normal obligation to accommodate any prisoner committed by the courts is another matter altogether. Against the background we have described, we do not see the public expenditure implications being so huge and concentrated in time that they necessarily provide a knock-down argument against piecemeal prison expansion to meet operational pressure. In our view, the ultimate accommodation constraints are less likely to be caused by public expenditure control than by the lead time before new prisons can be brought into use, and the extreme difficulty in finding practical and acceptable new sites in this crowded island. Even that constraint may come to look rather different. The more incarceration business that is put into the private sector, the more expertise will accumulate on getting the job done quickly (and, some may say, the more powerful the incarceration industry lobby that will be created, hungry for business).

Until there is a real shift towards lighter sentencing, the rising prison population will put increasingly intolerable pressure on the ability of even the best management to run the system in a sensible and humane way. That way is also the one that best protects the public by doing the maximum to encourage prisoners to address their offending behaviour and lead a law-abiding life. On the other hand, the efforts that will be made to find new accommodation will relentlessly increase the size of the system. The increased efficiency and security and control capability of the prison service, and the speed of construction and finance regime for private prisons, are radically new factors. Without some new component in the system, there must be a real risk that we shall be trapped in a ratcheting-up cycle, with high sentencing requiring more accommodation, which in turn attracts a further step in sentencing severity. There is no point in our trying to guess how far down this path the country might go, but both main political parties have clearly been much influenced by the recent politics of the USA. The one thing that could slow down the spiral would be for the government to inject an element of restraint into the situation, and that is the one thing against which the government has so far set its face.

We began this chapter by noting that the present developing crisis was set on course at the very moment when the pressure of prison numbers had only just eased, and the prison system was running at the capacity for which it was intended. That enabled several thousand prisoners to be squeezed into overcrowded conditions during the next few years. The most important lesson of the events since 1993 is just how vulnerable the entire system is to non-legislative pressure for ever higher retributive sentencing, once politi-cians choose to unleash that pressure. Until the previous government there had never been a time when the Prime Minister and Home Secretary of the

No real shift towards lighter sentencing!

day had actively encouraged more imprisonment and complained that the courts were too lenient. We do appear to be seeing a demonstration of things that academics have often asserted — that the prison population is essentially a matter of political choice, and that once political parties adopt rival policies of tough punishment, they will find themselves caught in the toils of a machine from which they cannot disengage. In the next section we consider whether there is any possible way of putting a brake on these dangers in the longer-term future.

A RESTRAINING PRINCIPLE

Most experts would say that informal social controls are far more important than the criminal justice system in controlling crime. Be that as it may, we are sure that there is an overwhelming consensus view among experts that what deterrent effect the system does have is related far more closely to the certainty of detection and enforcement than to the severity of punishment. The likelihood of detection has fallen hugely during the 1980s and 90s, and the weight of punishment has belatedly been pushed higher and higher. The situation is like a classroom in which the inadequate teacher, having lost order, is wildly overcompensating by threatening ever more extreme sanctions.

In this book we have touched on many different reasons why this country's apparently escalating high imprisonment policy simply does not add up to a sensible agenda. At this point we can summarise the case, as follows:

(a) Imprisonment is by far the most costly type of intervention, and the crime control effect of increasing already high imprisonment levels is marginal. This country had imprisonment rates that were high by Western European standards even before the present sentencing surge got under way.

(b) It goes without saying that offenders should be appropriately punished, and genuinely dangerous ones confined, but imprisonment is the worst possible thing that can lawfully be done to a person in this country and its effects are inherently likely to be deleterious. For that reason, until the time of 'Prison works' there was consensus agreement with the idea of restraint — only resorting to prison when unavoidable, and then for the shortest appropriate time. The current surge in sentencing seems to have lost contact with the principle of restraint.

(c) The amount of prison capacity is finite at any time, and it cannot be rapidly expanded. Pumping too many prisoners into the system is destructive of prison management, and makes imprisonment even more deleterious for prisoners. Anyone who has had any experience of an overcrowded prison system would take those points very seriously indeed. Without any other control, however, the provision of more accommodation is likely to attract yet more prisoners from the courts.

(d)   Finance to support decent prison regimes always comes *after* a rise in the prison population, and lags behind the need. There is no realistic likelihood of enough resources ever being released for additional prison places *and* for the provision of adequate regimes throughout the system.

(e)   In systems terms, the imprisonment of more adults for longer periods is simply the wrong place to spend money. As the government recognises, the criminal justice system has been tentative and ineffective with juveniles, giving them absolutely the wrong messages, but it is already severe with adult offenders.

(f)   In any event, money is most effectively spent outside the criminal justice system altogether, on crime prevention and on targeting the young people most at risk, and attempting to divert them from being sucked into crime in the first place.

It is not too difficult to state a rational aim for sentencing and the penal system, though the events described in part 2 show how extraordinarily difficult it is in practice to get anywhere near it. General policy should be established by Parliament; sentencing in individual cases should be left within the sentencer's discretion; and there should be sufficient harmonisation of aims between policy-makers and sentencers for the number of prisoners and people under probation supervision to be broadly consistent with the capacity of the penal system. That capacity must inevitably be decided by the government in the context of its public expenditure policy, and in any given period its limits can be defined quite accurately. During much of the 1980s the sentencers paid small regard to the capacity of the system; since 1993 it has been the two main political parties that have played down that constraint.

We are all familiar with the ideas of 'negative feedback' and 'positive feedback'. The thermostat on a domestic hot-water system is an example of 'negative feedback'; when the temperature of the water reaches the desired level, the thermostat cuts off the supply of heat until the system cools down sufficiently to require more heat to lift it back to the required temperature again. In 'positive feedback' exactly the opposite happens, so that each increase in heat (or speed, or pressure or whatever is being monitored) triggers off a demand for yet more heat (or speed or whatever) until the system reaches a point where equilibrium is established by some external agency or, of course, by self-destruction. Back in the 1970s, before the population explosion in American prisons, some academics in the USA developed the theory that self-regulatory characteristics were built in to the criminal justice system to prevent parts of it from exploding out of control, and they used the term 'homeostasis' to describe this. Not much is heard about homeostatic theory in the USA these days; the institutions that exercised a negative feedback effect have decayed; and all the political and other pressures are by way of positive feedback, for more and more and more punishment. The recent sentencing surge in this country has been so extreme, and there has been so little reasoned critique of it, that this country, too, has come perilously close to making the transition to positive feedback. We may, indeed, have done so.

The present Lord Chief Justice's principled expression of concern at recent sentencing trends may point the way to a more hopeful future. In the changed political climate on crime and punishment, though, it has obviously become very difficult for any government to show much recognition of the case for restraint or to try to 'talk the population down'. Politicians may have painted themselves into a corner, so that the one thing they find almost impossible to say is that less punishment is desirable. Without some new kind of restraining element, there must still be a real risk that we may see a USA-style escalation of imprisonment, and there is certainly no guarantee against that happening in the longer term. What restraining mechanism is feasible?

First and foremost, an extensive campaign of valid information is needed to displace the misconceptions and half-truths that are current about sentencing and the effectiveness of prison. Given the entrenched punitive attitude in much of the popular press, and without a body like a Royal Commission to do the job, this would be an extremely difficult thing to do. Nevertheless, it is essential. The government has made a start by deciding that the regular crime statistics should be presented in future by disinterested statisticians rather than by politicians, but much more needs to be done.

A significant step towards greater transparency and demystification was taken by the publication in January 1998 of a research study of public attitudes to punishment, based on interviews with around 8,000 respondents as part of the 1996 sweep of the British Crime Survey.[17] This found widespread ignorance among the public about crime and criminal justice, with the majority overestimating the gravity of crime problems and underestimating the severity of the criminal justice system. The report concluded that there was a crisis of confidence among sentencers, but that a policy of 'playing to the gallery' and further extending the use of imprisonment was not appropriate. Rather, modern public communication techniques should be exploited to convey an accurate portrayal of current sentencing practice to key audiences.

Straw welcomed the study and undertook that the government was committed to improving the information which the public receives about

---

[17] Hough, M. and Roberts, J., *Attitudes to punishment: findings from the British Crime Survey*, Home Office Research Study 179, London: Home Office, 1998.

crime and the criminal justice system. He said that the Home Office would be providing more comprehensive background information in its news releases. He also drew particular attention to the provisions in the Crime and Disorder Bill for the Court of Appeal to issue sentencing guidelines and to have the benefit of a new sentencing advisory panel. While this response is welcome as far as it goes, it only marks a beginning. Increasing the level of understanding of existing sentencing levels is in any event only one part of what needs to be done, and fuller departmental news releases could never themselves be more than a small component of the battery of overt political action that is required.

It is a trite observation that many of the problems in the criminal justice system flow from its fragmentation, and especially from the distinct and separate role of the sentencers. The mismatch that this causes between input and capacity has led to a long series of devices being proposed and attempted. All have failed. Adjusting the effect of sentences through parole was stretched beyond breaking point. The idea of a more principled sentencing framework collapsed in ruins. The Woolf Report's idea of capping the population of prisons was rejected out of hand. The Criminal Justice Consultative Council is not focused on the central issue. The Home Office's action over the years to encourage discussion between the component parts of the system has manifestly failed to affect sentencing, whatever other benefits there might have been. Against this background, it seems fanciful to suggest that we could be anywhere near the first steps towards ensuring that sentencing takes place within a matrix that is required to have some regard for the capacity of the penal system. It is just possible, however, that this could be in sight.

Interest is now concentrated on the government's proposals in the Crime and Disorder Bill for a new duty to be placed on the Court of Appeal to consider issuing sentencing guidelines when appropriate cases come before it or when it is recommended to do so by a new sentencing advisory panel. It is proposed that any new guidelines should have regard to:

    (a)   the need to promote greater consistency;
    (b)   current sentencing levels;
    (c)   the cost of different sentences and their relative effectiveness in preventing reoffending;
    (d)   the need to promote public confidence in the criminal justice system;
    (e)   the weight that should be given to previous convictions and response to previous sentences.

These proposals clearly open up the sentencing process to an unprecedented degree of outside involvement and informed input of different kinds. The need to be effective and prevent reoffending may lead to the commissioning of research in a way that could only be fruitful. The proposals have been broadly welcomed by the interest groups, and in the Bill's second reading in the House of Lords the Lord Chief Justice also indicated a generally favourable reaction, while questioning the propriety of requiring the Court to have regard to costs.[18]

All this has such a flavour of constructive dialogue and calm rationality that it seems churlish to suggest that the proposals have the look of having been put together so as to contain something for almost everybody, without hitting the bull's eye of the target. The role of the advisory panel is especially enigmatic at this stage. Although the Bill does not spell this out, Straw announced on 24 November 1997[19] that the panel would be expected to consult with representatives of various interested groups including police, probation and victims. There are obvious questions about the ability of even the most subtle panel to reflect a range of views that are bound to be highly divergent and the weight that the Court will be expected to give to the panel's advice is also unclear. In our view the one thing that is central to the long-term stability of the prison system and its ability to operate decently is to find an objectively-based restraining principle and this is conspicuously absent from the current proposals.

It is worth recalling at this point that, as Lord Bingham recognised in his July lecture, the Court's previous guidelines have mostly had the effect of raising sentences rather than lowering them, and we have already noted that the Court's composition and workload must steer it towards the top end of the sentencing tariff. While the proposed requirements would expose the Court of Appeal to a diffuse range of inputs, nothing in the proposed remit addresses head-on the one restraining factor that is immediately demonstrable, which is the capacity of the prisons and other parts of the penal system. We strongly believe that this is one of the matters that the Court should bear in mind.

It would not be helpful for a book of this kind to be too prescriptive about the way in which this kind of arrangement should be managed. That would be best left to the judiciary themselves. It would clearly not be at all sensible to think in terms of achieving a precise match of sentences and capacity, and neither could there be any question of being perceived to shorten sentences that are needed for public protection against violent and sex offenders. There should simply be an entrenched device that required the government to make periodic statements about the penal system's capacity and get some negative feedback into sentencing, especially for middle-rank offences of the kind Lord Bingham mentioned in his November lecture. The *Upton* and *Bibi*

---

[18] Hansard HL, 16 December 1997, col. 560–562.
[19] Hansard HC, 24 November 1997, col. 617.

judgments in 1980 already show that the Court knows how to take account of the prison situation if it wishes to do so.

The immediate question is the framing of the government's proposals for the Court of Appeal, but beyond this there are much deeper issues that will not go away. The criticism of the courts and the surge in sentencing since 1993 have been extraordinary events which require many of the old certainties to be reassessed. One thing that they have shown is how very easily general sentencing practice can be influenced — at least in an upward direction. The old protestations of the independent-minded sentencers seem a shade dated in the light of that experience. From the point of view of sentence providers, what the episode has shown is that the moment when the prison system's accommodation and population are in the balance is the moment of greatest vulnerability to demands for renewed, deliberate, overcrowding. Should the system become balanced again, there is nothing whatsoever to stop the episode being repeated endlessly.

Establishing a link between sentencing and penal system capacity would only be a moderating and stabilising device to avoid turbulence. Even a very generalised provision that sentencing guidelines should be prepared with a mind to capacity would do a lot to protect the position of the courts. There would be nothing unconstitutional about such a provision, alongside the others that are being proposed. It would be difficult for a political party, whether in government or not, to make unreasonable assertions about the alleged leniency of sentencing levels if such a provision was on the statute book and, once enacted, it would be politically difficult to repeal.

The events of the last few years have cruelly exposed the lack of any inbuilt machinery for balance and stability in the criminal justice system, and there is an opportunity to put it in place now.

The basic proposition in this book is that general sentencing policy, the capacity of the penal system and the level of overcrowding that is tolerated are all matters for political decision and management. The separate roles of judiciary and executive have, however, made it extremely hard for this obvious fact to be recognised. Indeed, it may well have served the interests of both parties to the argument for the issue to be obscured. Now that it has been shown how easily the sentencers can be influenced without even involving the process of parliamentary sanction through legislation, the political nature of the ultimate responsibility has surely become much plainer.

As Lord Bingham has pointed out, it is a novel proposition that sentencers should have regard to the relative costs of sentences as one of their main concerns. To our minds, that genuinely contentious requirement distracts attention from the immediate and practical problem, which is that sentencing should take place in a framework that at least acknowledges the consequences of governmental resource planning as expressed by the capacity of the penal system on the ground. The two issues are not the same.

The proposals in the Crime and Disorder Bill, as currently formulated, mean that the Court of Appeal is to have the benefit of generalised inputs from almost every quarter except the government itself. That certainly pays homage to the independence of the judiciary and the separation of powers, but there is surely something strange about a set of inputs that is so remarkably coy about the capacity of the system and the government's responsibility for it. It is quite proper that the capacity of the penal system should be settled through the political process, and the way to reflect that would be for a statement of capacity (subject to an appropriate parliamentary procedure) to be included in the matters for which the Court should have regard.

While we believe that the entrenchment of a restraining principle in legislation would have a unique long term importance, the immediate factors (as always) are the approach to public opinion and the signals that are sent to sentencers. During the last few years the political system took several highly visible and violent blows at the sentencing process. We are frankly doubtful whether any less vigorous and direct commitment by government will be sufficient to counter-act the effects of this.

The case for restraint in the use of imprisonment is not a matter that requires more research before it can be confidently stated: the facts about imprisonment's cost and its marginal crime-control effect have been well understood for years. Neither can there be any serious question about the inherent tendency of prisons to be damaging places. It is no more than common sense to say that a constantly overstretched prison system is unlikely to operate in a way that lives up to its aspirations of discouraging reoffending. There is absolutely no reason to expect that new bodies could establish these matters in the public mind in a way that the government itself is somehow debarred from doing.

As this book goes to press the government is considering its response to Lord Ackner's proposal that a body similar to the old Advisory Council on the Penal System (ACPS) should be set up to advise the Home Secretary. This was debated by the House of Lords as an amendment to the Crime and Disorder Bill on 3 March 1998, when the government spokesman undertook that the proposal would be considered, while pointing out the range of sources from which information was already available. We would certainly not want to argue against the idea of a reconstituted ACPS, which could have a useful part to play within a wider strategy, but such a body could not of itself do a great deal to address public opinion and set an agenda. The real question is whether the government is content to see our prison system continue to expand beyond Western European norms, or whether it really wishes to do something about it.

Index

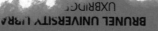